THE $650 BILLION BARGAIN

THE MARSHALL PAPERS

After World War II, Brookings scholars played an instrumental role in helping the United States craft a concept of international order and build a set of supporting institutions, including what became known as the Marshall Plan in honor of Secretary of State George C. Marshall, who spearheaded the effort. Now, a generation later, the Brookings Foreign Policy program, as part of the Order from Chaos project, has launched a new book series—The Marshall Papers—evoking that vital historical juncture. These short monographs will provide accessible, long-form research on critical international questions designed to stimulate debate about how the United States and others should act to promote an international order that continues to foster peace, prosperity, and justice.

THE MARSHALL PAPERS

THE $650 BILLION BARGAIN

THE CASE FOR MODEST GROWTH IN AMERICA'S DEFENSE BUDGET

MICHAEL E. O'HANLON

BROOKINGS INSTITUTION PRESS

Washington, D.C.

Copyright © 2016
THE BROOKINGS INSTITUTION
1775 Massachusetts Avenue, N.W., Washington, D.C. 20036
www.brookings.edu

The Brookings Institution is a private nonprofit organization devoted to research, education, and publication on important issues of domestic and foreign policy. Its principal purpose is to bring the highest quality independent research and analysis to bear on current and emerging policy problems. Interpretations or conclusions in Brookings publications should be understood to be solely those of the authors.

Library of Congress Cataloging-in-Publication data
Names: O'Hanlon, Michael E., author.
Title: The $650 billion bargain : the case for modest growth in America's defense budget / Michael E. O'Hanlon.
Description: Washington, D.C. : Brookings Institution Press, [2016] | Series: The Marshall papers | Includes bibliographical references and index.
Identifiers: LCCN 2016017490 (print) | LCCN 2016018468 (ebook) | ISBN 9780815729570 (pbk.) | ISBN 9780815729587 (ebook)
Subjects: LCSH: National security—United States—Finance. | United States—Armed Forces—Appropriations and expenditures. | United States. Department of Defense—Appropriations and expenditures. | United States—Military policy. | Budget—United States.
Classification: LCC UA23 .O343 2016 (print) | LCC UA23 (ebook) | DDC 355.6/22973—dc23
LC record available at https://lccn.loc.gov/2016017490

9 8 7 6 5 4 3 2 1

Typeset in Minion

Composition by Westchester Publishing Services

Contents

Preface

Today the United States budgets just over $600 billion a year for its national defense. That is a great deal of money. It is roughly the right amount, however. And in fact, it should increase modestly under the next president—with budget authority totaling about $650 billion, and outlays or spending remaining near 3 percent of GDP. (By way of comparison, in 2016, national defense spending represents 3.2 percent of GDP and in 2017 it is projected to total 3.1 percent, but under President Obama's 2017 budget request it would drop to 2.7 percent in 2020 and 2.6 percent in 2021).[1]

President Obama's last fiscal projections would have the national defense budget decline from $607 billion in 2016 to about $575 billion in 2020, expressed in constant 2016 figures. That assumes roughly flat real-dollar funding for the base or core budget of the Department of Defense, together with a far greater reduction in war costs over the next few years than is realistic. Indeed, Mr. Obama assumes that overseas contingency operations budgets will decline from $59 billion in 2017 to no more than $11 billion in 2018. My proposal would envision a national defense budget around

$650 billion in 2020—with a large part of the discrepancy, roughly $50 billion each year, resulting from my assumption that overseas contingency operations (OCO) costs will remain around their current level. In the meantime, national defense budgets would be about $615 billion for 2016 (meaning an additional supplement for the current fiscal year), and $625 billion for 2017, growing gradually to $650 billion by 2020. Once expected inflation is factored in, that latter number would equal about $700 billion in nominal (or actual) dollar terms.

My recommended increases would differ with the Obama administration's last budget in two other main ways. First, they would be designed to address a mismatch between ends and means in the Pentagon's current plans; right now, as is usually the case, the Pentagon is planning to buy more weapons and sustain more force structure than projected budgets can really afford. This problem is seen vividly in the Fiscal Year 2017 budget request, which cuts about $11 billion in planned buys of equipment as foreseen for that 2017 budget a year earlier.[2] The Pentagon was not able to buy the weapons it previously thought it needed under a binding ceiling for 2017, and it accordingly reduced planned procurement in response.[3] At least the Pentagon is rightly prioritizing long-term research and development and protecting that part of the budget, as it should, while also devoting adequate resources to security crises in Europe and the Middle East. But the structural funding shortfall persists beyond 2017.

Second, my recommendations would end cuts to the U.S. Army and retain an active-duty force of some 470,000 soldiers rather than the planned figure of 450,000. These two changes would add some $30 billion to the annual budget.

In the pages that follow, I argue for certain reforms, efficiencies, and cutbacks as well. Specifically, I advocate policy and programmatic changes that by 2020 could produce $2 billion annually in reductions in tactical aircraft acquisition, several billion in nuclear weapons accounts, up to $5 billion in military compensation accounts, and up to $2 billion more in management reforms such as greater use of performance-based logistics. Collectively, these could exceed $10 billion a year in savings. But many are controversial, and most would be slow to produce savings—perhaps slower than I have projected. As such, their combined, cumulative short-term effect on the budget would be important but modest, and not enough to rebut the argument in favor of modest, sustained real increases in the national security budget.

Indeed, having proposed adding some $2.5 billion to both its European Reassurance Initiative *and* its warfighting budget against the so-called Islamic State in Iraq and the Levant (ISIL) in the 2017 budget, the Obama administration has funded the so-called Overseas Contingency Operations accounts in 2017 less robustly than it had in 2016.[4] The administration has also added several billion dollars to cybersecurity funding for the Department of Defense. Thus, my recommendation on that front, which echoes arguments of some key Republican members of Congress, should not even await the presidential election; it should be enacted right away. In fact, unless some of the base-budget costs now being funded out of OCO accounts can be moved back into the regular base budget, 2016 OCO funding should probably be increased by nearly $10 billion to account for the increased pace of activities from Libya to Iraq and Syria to Afghanistan that the Obama administration should implement. The 2017 OCO figures also need to increase to account for a somewhat larger effort than planned (or currently in place) in Afghanistan and Syria, and perhaps other places as well.

My recommended increases are not as large as some reputable scholars, and a notable recent commission, have advocated. By way of comparison, the independent and nonpartisan 2014 National Defense Panel favors a force that could cost $675 billion, in constant-dollar terms. So would some of the 2016 presidential candidates. Indeed, by way of illustration, it is quite reasonable to make a case for at least two defense initiatives that would each raise the steady-state annual defense budget by $5 billion to $15 billion more than I have proposed (in other words, leaving it permanently higher by that amount). First, the size of the active-duty U.S. Army could be restored to closer to its 1990s levels; that would amount to a roughly 5 percent increase in size and cost relative to today (and 10 percent greater than currently planned Obama administration levels for later in the decade). Second, U.S. Navy shipbuilding might be increased by, say, half to two-thirds—from an expected average of about nine ships a year to around fifteen or so. That would also restore the Navy to 1990s levels by the end of the next president's would-be second term. It would increase the U.S. lead over China's navy, at least in terms of fleet tonnage, and thus further undergird the military requirements of the so-called Asia-Pacific rebalance concept of President Obama. However, given the country's fiscal condition and also its substantial military capabilities at present, I do not favor these additional measures for now. Moreover, the Department of Defense should remain under some pressure to make tough choices and necessary reforms.

TABLE 1-1. *Reference Points on U.S. National Defense Budgets*
Constant, 2016 dollars (rounded)

Year or period	Budget
Reference points	
Cold War Average, 1951–1990	$525
Reagan peak	$640
2000	$440
Bush/Obama peak	$780
Recent and projected numbers	
2016	$607
2017	$610
Obama budget, 2020	$575
Sequestration level, 2020	$555
Recommendations	
2014 National Defense Panel	$675
O'Hanlon proposal	$650

Note: These figures include all relevant war costs and Department of Energy nuclear weapons activities; they do not include funds for the Department of Homeland Security, Department of Veterans Affairs, or security assistance programs within the purview of the Department of State.

Acknowledgments

I am indebted to a wide range of colleagues, especially at Brookings but also beyond, in writing this book. Working at a defense center embedded in one of the best foreign policy programs at any think tank or university in the country has been an extraordinary privilege. It has helped me greatly with the tour d'horizon of the world's countries and likely future hotspots that was integral to the methodology of this project.

I would like to begin by thanking the Brookings defense team of 2016: John Allen, Robert Einhorn, Vanda Felbab-Brown, Bruce Riedel, Steven Pifer, Ian Livingston and Brendan Orino, Bradley Porter and James Tyson, as well as Che Bolden, Garrett Campbell, Barry Huggins, Chris Mac-Aulay, Dave Mastro, Frances Messalle, Tony Schinella, and Hiroyuki Sugai.

Bruce Jones is leading the Foreign Policy program with vision, collegiality, inspiration, and compassion, with Charlotte Baldwin as his talented and dedicated wingwoman. Strobe Talbott has been a collegial and brilliant leader of the institution for more than a dozen years. I have also been privileged to have as colleagues Tanvi Madan, Steve Cohen, Cliff Gaddy, Harold Trinkunas, Richard Bush, Jeff Bader, Ken Lieberthal, David Dollar, Martin Indyk, Jonathan Pollack, Kenneth Pollack, Kathy Moon, Mireya Solis, Dan Byman, Tamara Wittes, Shadi Hamid, Salman Shaikh, Ye Qi, Jeremy Shapiro, Tom Wright, Bob Kagan, Fiona Hill, Beth Ferris, Suzanne Maloney, Charley Ebinger, Charlotte Baldwin, Julia Cates, Nicki Sullivan, David Wessel, Alice Rivlin, Ron Haskins, Bill Gale, Bill Galston, Phil Gordon, Amy Liu, Mark Muro, Bruce Katz, William Antholis, Steven Bennett, Gail Chalef, Elisa Glazer, Emily Perkins, Peter Toto, Sadie Jonath, Maggie Humenay, Ben Cahen, Doug Elmendorf, Karen Dynan, Lois Rice, Susan Rice, Roberta Cohen, Ted Piccone, E.J. Dionne, Tom Mann, Steve Hess, Marvin Kalb, Barry Bosworth, Henry Aaron, and many others.

Beyond Brookings, my debts extend to many more, starting with Jim Steinberg and including Michael Doran, Peter Singer, Aaron Friedberg, John Ikenberry, Hal Feiveson, Frank von Hippel, Kim and Fred Kagan, Mackenzie Eaglen, Tom Donnelly, Michele Flournoy, Jim Miller, Kurt Campbell, Eric Edelman, Steve Solarz, Eliot Cohen, Vali Nasr, Steve Biddle, Max Boot, Michael Levi, Tom Christensen, Janine Davidson, Janne Nolan, Dick Betts, Ari Roth, Bruce Klingner, Bud Cole, Kathleen Hicks, Tony Cordesman, John Hamre, Eliot Cohen, Juan Carlos Pinzon, Diana Quintera, John Sattler, Ron Neumann, John Nagl, Duncan Brown, Larry Korb, David Gordon, Todd Harrison, Andrew Krepinevich, Frank Hoffman, Josh Epstein, Paul Stares, Tom McNaugher, Mike Mochizuki, Nick Lardy, David Shambaugh, Ashley Tellis, Michael Swaine, Karim Sadjapour, Ben Lambeth, Sean Zeigler, Andy Hoehn, Jim Dobbins, Mike Armacost, Bruce MacLaury, John Steinbruner, Carlos Pascual, Richard Haass, Jim Lindsay, Ivo Daalder, Barry Posen, Dave Petraeus, Stan

McChrystal, Mike Meese, Barry McCaffrey, Maya Mac-
Guineas, Woody Turner, Rebecca Grant, Bob Haffa, Richard
Fontaine, Dan Benjamin, Kori Schake, Steve Hadley, Paul
Wolfowitz, Robert Reischauer, Robert Hale, Jack Mayer,
Wayne Glass, Neil Singer, Dave Mosher, Fran Lussier, Lane
Pierrot, Michael Berger, Ellen Breslin Davidson, my many
students over the years, and many members of Congress and
the Executive Branch who have inspired and/or taught me
as well. Finally, I am deeply grateful to the members of
Brookings's national security industrial base project, and to
Herb and Herbert Allen as well as many other members and
supporters within the Brookings family.

The Foreign Policy program is grateful to Danny Abraham,
Jonathan Colby, Raj Fernando, Ben Jacobs, Ned Lamont,
and Haim Saban for their generous support of this Marshall
Paper, which is part of the larger Order from Chaos project.
Brookings recognizes that the value it provides is in its
absolute commitment to quality, independence, and impact.
Activities supported by its donors reflect this commitment.

CHAPTER 1

State of the Security Environment—and the Purposes of American Power

Before getting into a detailed discussion of forces, weapons, capabilities, and deployments, it is important to ask—what are the purposes of U.S. military power?

When there is an acute and obvious threat to the nation, as in World War II, the answer to this question can become obvious. More often than not, however, the threats are distant, diffuse, or nascent, and the question is difficult. Indeed, even in World War II, the United States needed to decide on the proper ordering of its efforts, electing to focus first on Europe. Even in the Cold War, it took many years to figure out how to implement the military dimensions of containment policy through means such as the NATO alliance and the creation of the U.S. Armed Forces' overseas command structures.

Since the Cold War ended, the task has not gotten any easier. The absence of a single overriding threat may have made the world less acutely dangerous, yet it has complicated the task of strategists and military planners. On balance, I would say that this is a good problem to have. Nostalgia for the Cold War, and remembrances of its supposed stability, are often overdone. But the complexity of today's international security environment nonetheless poses a challenge.

A number of concepts have been advanced in an attempt to provide a unifying purpose to America's role in the post-Cold War world and, by extension, its military strategy. President George H. W. Bush spoke of a new world order, and reversed Iraq's invasion of Kuwait to uphold it. President Bill Clinton had a national security strategy of engagement and enlargement, which led to the expansion of NATO and numerous peacekeeping missions in places like the Balkans. President George W. Bush responded to 9/11 with the concept of preemption and emphasis on a "balance of power that favors freedom"—in many ways a new slogan for America's longstanding interest in promoting democracy. Barack Obama, chastened by the Bush experiences and later the unfolding of the so-called Arab spring, has placed less emphasis on classic foreign policy matters, attempting to focus more on global issues such as climate change as well as the domestic agenda. In fact, through it all, U.S. military strategy and posture have not changed radically from one administration to the next during the quarter century since the Cold War ended. But there is a fair amount of churn in the conceptual underpinnings of American grand strategy—and a real challenge for the next president about how to describe his or her core national security tenets and policies.

The best way to get at the question of American grand strategy is to take stock of the character of the international security environment today. The United States is interested, in the first instance, in protecting its own people and territory from acts of aggression. But it also has sought to foster a global order in which key overseas allies and interests are protected, in the interest of broader American security and prosperity, and in awareness of the fact that ignoring problems abroad has generally hurt U.S. security. (The United States tried a policy of non-interference, related to today's academically popular paradigm of offshore balancing, before both world wars and to some extent the Korean war.) There are problems with this overall narrative, to be sure, as the Bernie Sanders and Donald Trump campaigns in the United States have helped reveal in 2015 and 2016. For one thing, the United States spends a higher share of its gross domestic product on its military than almost all of its allies and security partners, raising valid questions about burden-sharing. Yet these issues are no more acute than during the Cold War and indeed, on balance they are probably less concerning now, given that American military spending has dropped to a modest share of the nation's economic output. A larger problem is that, even though America as a nation has never been richer, members of its middle economic classes often feel disempowered and disenfranchised by the forces of globalization. They also feel poorer and less secure than before, and less hopeful about the future. Sustaining support for American internationalism therefore undoubtedly requires significant steps to make the middle classes more supportive of such a goal—which in turn has repercussions for tax policy (and the progressivity of the tax code), for education policy, and for the labor provisions of trade agreements among other matters in public policy.

All that said, the internationalist role of the United States has been on balance very beneficial, and it is important to recognize as much. Indeed, despite the recent bedlam affecting the Middle East in particular, overall trends in human history have been clearly favorable in recent decades.[1] The overall frequency of interstate violence has declined greatly.

Casualties from all types of war, particularly when adjusted for the size of the human population, are down substantially. Prosperity has extended to many corners of the world that were previously extremely poor.

Of course, there is much left to do, and much that can still go wrong. Deterrence can still fail owing to misperception about commitments, the ascent to power of risk-prone leaders in key nations, enduring historical grievances that resurface at a future date after a period of quiet, and disputes over resources of one type or another.[2] Here we should think of Vladimir Putin and his recent behavior, or the leadership of Iran, or the ongoing rivalries between the Koreas and between India and Pakistan.

Moreover, there have been more than thirty civil wars at any given point during much of the twenty-first century. This remains a higher figure than in much of the twentieth century.[3] Estimated fatalities from those wars, typically 20,000 to 40,000 annually in recent years, and perhaps twice as great since 2011, are substantially less than from the civil wars of the late 1970s, 1980s, and early 1990s but not appreciably less than those from the 1950s and certain other periods. In other words, there may be a generally hopeful trend toward decreased global violence, but it is hardly so pronounced or so definitive as to foretell an obsolescence of armed conflict.[4] Moreover, civil wars are very difficult to resolve definitively, and often recur even after peace accords are in place.[5]

There were still some seventeen UN peace operations globally as of 2014, involving more than 100,000 personnel in total. Additional non-UN missions continue in other countries. Total numbers of peacekeepers, under UN auspices and otherwise, have consistently grown in this century even without counting the Afghanistan operation.[6] In places such as Syria and Iraq, serious violence continues. Largely as a result, world totals for refugees and internally displaced persons (IDPs) remain high. More than 10 million refugees are under the care of the UN High Commissioner for Refugees (down from an early 1990s peak of 18 million but much greater than 1960s and 1970s totals), with the largest numbers from Afghanistan, Syria, Somalia, Sudan, and the Democratic Republic of Congo. These same countries along with Colombia, have large numbers of IDPs as well. Indeed, global totals for IDPs are at historic highs. All told, forced displacement in recent years topped 50 million globally for the first time since World War II.[7]

Terrorism has increased dramatically in this century by comparison with the latter decades of the twentieth century.[8] Some extremist movements are now able to hide away within the world's great and growing megalopolises to a greater extent than many previous insurgent or rebellious movements in history. In so doing, they can gain access to information, communications, transportation systems, funding, and recruits.[9] President Obama frequently talked about al Qaeda or ISIL being on the run or on the path to defeat in 2012, 2013, and 2014. But that optimism was premature at best. It could really only be said to apply to the traditional core of the organization that attacked the United States in 2001,[10] and perhaps now to the core of ISIL within Iraq and Syria as the group started to clearly lose ground by late 2015 in these areas. Al Qaeda affiliates remain active in dozens of countries. ISIL has now gained adherents from Nigeria and Libya to the Sinai to Afghanistan while continuing to attract many recruits to the Middle East—and to inspire terrible attacks around the world.[11]

In regard to the so-called democratic peace, it is true that established, functioning constitutional democracies fight each other much less often, statistically speaking.[12] It is also true that such countries are becoming more common, with about 120 countries, or nearly two-thirds of the nations of the planet, electoral democracies by the turn of the twenty-first century. However, even such countries are not impervious to the possibility of civil war (as the American Civil War showed), or to a possible coup or hijacking by a strongman, who then misrules the state (as Hitler's hijacking of the Weimar Republic demonstrates), or to other aberrations. The extraordinary popularity of Vladimir Putin in Russia since 2014, even if partly fabricated and engineered by the Kremlin, should alone throw some cold water on any excessive optimism about the hypothesis that the trappings of democracy will automatically produce naturally peaceful nations. Egypt's extremely turbulent recent history provides another timely reminder. Democratic peace theory may work well for established, inclusive, constitutional democracies based on the liberal principle of the rights and worth of the individual. However, such states are rarer than are electoral democracies in general, and not yet sufficiently widespread for the planet to depend on any particular system of governance to ensure the peace.[13]

UN peacekeeping operations are prevalent in today's world, as noted, and are worthy enterprises in most cases. But they still fail perhaps 40 percent of the time; some conflicts are just too deeply rooted, or the world's collective peacekeeping and conflict resolution capacities are too lacking, to do better than that. This is not an argument against such missions—which do in fact succeed in whole or part some 60 percent of the time.[14] But it should remind us that, as in most things, change is often slow and uneven.

The notion that nuclear deterrence has created a world in which major powers are less likely to engage in all-out war against each other is probably true. However, nuclear deterrence would seem less dependable in cases where states consider or engage in limited war (which may or may not remain limited once they start) or in situations in which one of them has a disproportionately greater interest than the other in regard to the issue that precipitated the crisis at hand and is therefore willing to risk brinkmanship, in the belief the other side will blink first. Conflicts can also erupt in which renegade local commanders may have their own agendas, or in which command and control systems for nuclear weapons are less than fully dependable.[15] Moreover, the history of nuclear deterrence has not been as easy or as happy as some nostalgically remember it being. There were near misses during the Cold War, with the Berlin and Cuban missile crises. The spread of nuclear capabilities in places such as South Asia and the Middle East increases the odds that the tradition of nuclear nonuse may not survive indefinitely.[16]

Then there is the hope that economic interdependence and globalization will make the idea of warfare so irrational and unappealing as to ensure no major conflict among the great economies of the world. There is indeed some basis for this observation. Alas, nations historically have proven able to convince themselves that future wars will be short (and victorious), allowing for the creation of narratives about how conflict would not preclude prosperity. Also, joint economic interests among nations have existed for centuries, even as war has continued; international trade and investment were strong just before the outbreak of World War I, for example.[17]

On balance, it is probably true that major war in today's world has become less likely as a result of the sum total of nuclear deterrence, the spread of democracies, globalization, and other factors, including awareness of the destructiveness of modern conventional weaponry as well.[18] But that provides no grounds for complacency. The overall chances of war could be lower than before and the duration of time between catastrophic wars longer, yet the potential damage from conflict could be so great that war might remain just as much a threat to humankind in the future as it has been in the past. For example, even a small-scale nuclear war in a heavily populated part of the planet could wreak untold havoc, and decimate infrastructure that might take years to repair, with huge second-order effects on human well-being for tens of millions of individuals. Biological pathogens far more destructive than the generally noncontagious varieties that have been known to date could be invented (also superbugs could develop naturally, for example through mutations). And the effects of climate change on a very densely populated globe could have enormous implications for the physical safety and security of tens of millions as well, causing new conflicts or intensifying existing ones. The case for hope about the future course of the world is fairly strong—but it is a case for hope, not a guarantee.[19]

And that hope for a better future is almost surely more credible with a strong United States. To be sure, there are differences of opinion over how U.S. strategic leadership should be exercised. Some do express concern that specific mistakes in U.S. foreign policy could lead to war.[20] There is also disagreement over whether the concepts of American primacy and exceptionalism are good guides to future U.S. foreign policy.[21] But there is little reason to believe that a truly multipolar world would be safer than, or inherently preferable to, today's system, or that a different leader besides the United States would do a better job organizing international cooperative behavior among nations.

Today, the United States leads a coalition or loose alliance system of some sixty states that together account for some 70 percent of world military spending (and a similar fraction of total world GDP). This is extraordinary in the history of nations, especially by comparison with most of European history of the last several centuries, when variable power balances and shifting alliances were the norm. Even in the absence of a single, clear threat, the NATO alliance, major bilateral East Asian alliances, major Middle Eastern and Persian Gulf security partnerships, and the Rio Pact have endured. To be sure, this Western-led system is under stress and challenge. Yet it remains strong—and at least as appealing to most rising powers as does any alternative political or economic model.

What this long discussion is meant to achieve is an analytical rationale for a U.S. military that remains engaged globally in protecting the so-called commons (international air and sea zones, that is), partnering with allies to enhance their security, deterring great-power conflict, and constraining proliferation where possible. Ideally, it would also contribute to urgent humanitarian needs when others cannot provide them alone, such as prevention of genocide or provision of humanitarian relief. In other words, it should continue to uphold the international order, working with allies and employing other elements of national power in the process. Coupled with an economic strategy that has fostered international trade and investment, and a diplomatic strategy that has favored inclusiveness for all nations, such an American foreign policy has since World War II helped facilitate the greatest progress in the well-being of humans in the history of the planet. Correctly applied, it is also the best strategy to prevent the rise of a hostile power and the prospect of a World War III, and to minimize the dangers of nuclear proliferation as well.

CHAPTER 2

The U.S. Defense Budget in Perspective

Before launching into detailed policy proposals, some defense basics are useful to keep in mind. Today's American armed forces are relatively modest in size by most measures—though they are also fairly expensive, as will be discussed further below.

PERSONNEL AND FORCE STRUCTURE

The Department of Defense's total active-duty uniformed personnel number some 1.3 million. These totals are down from late Cold-War totals of more than 2 million uniformed personnel, and from Clinton-era figures of around 1.4 million. Another 800,000 reservists and 775,000 full-time civilian employees of the department round out the official workforce (not counting contractors). The 2020 U.S. Army will have some 450,000 soldiers and thirty brigade combat teams in the active force (it will have twenty-six more brigade combat teams in the National Guard). The Navy plans

TABLE 2-1. *Major Elements of U.S. Military Force Structure, 2017*

Category	Capability
Nuclear Forces	14 SSBNs, 450 ICBMs
Bombers	96 operational aircraft, 58 additional
Navy	287 ships (11 large-deck aircraft carriers), building to 308 by 2021 (with 11 carriers still)
Air Force Tactical Fighter Squadrons	55
Army Brigade Combat Teams	30 in active force, 26 in National Guard
Army Combat Aviation Brigades	11 in active force, 10 in Guard/ Reserve
Army Soldiers	450,000 active by 2018; 530,000 Guard/Reserve
United States Marine Corps Infantry Battalions	24
Marines	182,000 active; 39,000 Reserve
Air Force Uniformed Personnel	317,000 active; 174,000 Guard/ Reserve
Navy Sailors	323,000 active; 59,000 Reserve

Source: Office of the Under Secretary of Defense (Comptroller), "Fiscal Year 2017 Budget Request: Briefing Slides," Department of Defense, February 2016, available at comptroller.defense.gov/budgetmaterials/budget2017.aspx; and Office of the Under Secretary of Defense (Comptroller), "Fiscal Year 2017 Budget Request: Overview," Department of Defense, February 2016, p. A-1, available at http://comptroller.defense.gov/Portals/45/Documents/defbudget /fy2017/FY2017_Budget_Request_Overview_Book.pdf.

Note: SSBNs are ballistic-missile submarines; ICBMs are intercontinental-range ballistic missiles.

to grow modestly by 2021 to a fleet of 308 ships, including eleven large-deck aircraft carriers and fourteen ballistic-missile submarines. The Air Force will operate fifty-five squadrons of tactical fighter aircraft and almost 100 bombers (out of slightly more than 150 in the total inventory) as well as 450 ICBMs (headed to 400 by 2018, when the New START Treaty provisions come fully into effect). The Marine Corps, at 182,000 active-duty uniformed strength, will continue to maintain three divisions and three associated air wings.

Of the requested $534 billion in base budget for 2016, some $210 billion was planned for operations and maintenance, nearly another $140 billion for military personnel compensation, almost $110 billion for procurement, and $70 billion for research, development, testing, and evaluation (with small amounts for construction and housing). Broken down a different way, that $534 billion was allocated as follows: $161 billion for the Navy (including the Marine Corps); $127 billion for the Army; $153 billion for the Air Force (including many intelligence-related expenditures, since the U.S. intelligence budget of some $70 billion is hidden throughout the defense budget), and almost $95 billion for defense-wide activities or organizations.

IS U.S. DEFENSE SPENDING HIGH OR LOW?

It is possible to make the case that today's U.S. defense budget is either very big or quite modest and affordable. In fact, there are elements of reasonableness in either interpretation—and it is worth spelling those out. Those who claim that America is hypermilitarized, on the one hand, or that it is somehow dismantling its military on the other, are overstating their respective cases.

FIGURE 2-1. *U.S. National Defense Annual Budget Outlays, FY 1962–2021*

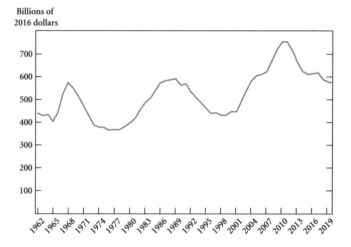

Billions of
2016 dollars

Sources: White House Office of Management and Budget, *Historical Tables: Budget of the U.S. Government, FY2017* (Washington, D.C., February 2016), Table 8.2; U.S. Bureau of Labor Statistics, "CPI Inflation Calculator," http:// data.bls.gov/cgi-bin/cpicalc.pl

Note: Figures are based on the president's budget request for 2017. Totals include all war and enacted supplemental funding and include Department of Energy national security spending. Estimates begin in 2016.

For those who complain about an American military in decline—or even one that has supposedly been "eviscerated" or "destroyed" by President Obama, a few basic figures should help calm down the hyperbole. America's current national defense budget of just over $600 billion a year (in constant, inflation-adjusted 2016 dollars, as are all figures in this paper) exceeds the Cold-War average for the United States of about $525 billion in those same, constant dollars. It greatly exceeds the Year 2000 level, just before the 9/11 attacks, of somewhat over $400 billion.[1] The U.S. national defense budget, which does not include budgets for Veterans Affairs or the Depart-

TABLE 2-2. *Global Distribution of Military Spending, 2015*

Country	Defense expenditure (millions of current \$)	Percent of global total	Cumulative percentage
United States	597,503	38.3	38
FORMAL U.S. ALLIES			
NATO			
Canada	14,007	0.9	39
France	46,751	3.0	42
Germany	36,686	2.3	45
Italy	21,552	1.4	46
Spain	10,754	0.7	47
Turkey	8,347	0.5	47
United Kingdom	56,244	3.6	51
Rest of NATO[a]	48,451	3.1	54
Total NATO (excluding U.S.)	242,792	15.5	
Total NATO	840,295	53.8	
Rio Pact[b]	52,366	3.4	57
KEY ASIA-PACIFIC ALLIES			
Japan	41,013	2.6	60
South Korea	33,460	2.1	62
Australia	22,764	1.5	63
New Zealand	2,418	0.2	64
Thailand	5,374	0.3	64
Philippines	2,223	0.1	64
Total key Asia-Pacific allies	107,252	6.9	
INFORMAL U.S. ALLIES			
Israel	18,597	1.2	65
Egypt	6,394	0.4	66
Iraq	21,100	1.4	67

(continued)

TABLE 2-2. *(continued)*

	Defense expenditure (millions of current $)	Percent of global total	Cumulative percentage
Country			
Pakistan	7,456	0.5	68
Gulf Cooperation Council[c]*	116,297	7.4	75
Jordan	1,603	0.1	75
Morocco	3,298	0.2	75
Mexico	6,051	0.4	76
Taiwan	10,257	0.7	76
Total informal allies	191,053	12.2	
OTHER NATIONS			
Non-NATO Europe	17,499	1.1	77
Other Middle East and North Africa[d]*	19,754	1.3	78
Other Central and South Asia[e]*	12,007	0.8	79
Other East Asia and Pacific[f]	21,880	1.4	81
Other Caribbean and Latin America[g]*	289	0.0	81
Sub-Saharan Africa	21,648	1.4	82
Total other nations	93,077	6.0	
MAJOR NEUTRAL NATIONS			
China	145,832	9.3	92
Russia	51,605	3.3	95
India	47,965	3.1	98
Indonesia	7,587	0.5	98
Total major neutral nations	252,989	16.2	

TABLE 2-2.

NEMESES AND ADVERSARIES

Iran*	15,862	1.0	99
North Korea[h]	5,000	0.3	100
Syria*	2,300	0.1	100
Venezuela	1,205	0.1	100
Cuba*	100	0.0	100
Total nemeses and adversaries	24,467		
TOTAL	1,561,499	100.0	100

Source: International Institute for Strategic Studies, *The Military Balance 2016* (New York: Routledge Press, 2016), pp. 484–490.

a. Albania, Belgium, Bulgaria, Croatia, Czech Republic, Denmark, Estonia, Greece, Hungary, Iceland, Latvia, Lithuania, Luxembourg, Netherlands, Norway, Poland, Portugal, Romania, Slovakia, and Slovenia.

b. Argentina, Bahamas, Bolivia, Brazil, Chile, Colombia, Costa Rica, Dominican Republic, Ecuador, El Salvador, Guatemala, Haiti, Honduras, Nicaragua, Panama, Paraguay, Peru, Trinidad and Tobago, and Uruguay.

c. Bahrain, Kuwait, Oman, Qatar, Saudi Arabia, and United Arab Emirates.

d. Algeria, Lebanon, Libya, Mauritania, Tunisia, and Yemen.

e. Afghanistan, Bangladesh, Kazakhstan, Kyrgyzstan, Nepal, Sri Lanka, Tajikistan, Turkmenistan, and Uzbekistan.

f. Brunei, Cambodia, Fiji, Laos, Malaysia, Mongolia, Myanmar, Papua New Guinea, Singapore, Timor Leste, and Vietnam.

g. Antigua and Barbuda, Barbados, Belize, Guyana, Jamaica, and Suriname.

h. North Korea value is an author estimate. Some estimates for China approach $200 billion.

* Calculation partly based on numbers from 2013 or 2014 because 2015 data are not available.

ment of Homeland Security (but does include Department of Energy nuclear weapons expenses as well as most intelligence accounts), remains a full 35 percent of world military spending. America's allies and close friends account for almost as much between them, meaning that the western alliance system wields the preponderance of global military resources even in the context of China's rise and Russia's revanchism.

Individual parts of the defense budget are reasonably healthy, too. Military compensation easily exceeds the average for the American workforce for individuals of given age, education, and experience across the preponderance of military specialties. Weapons budgets are not quite what they were under Ronald Reagan but still exceed $100 billion a year; the so-called "procurement holiday" of the 1990s and early 2000s is over. Funds for training are roughly adequate for the size of the force, akin to Reagan-era levels as well in terms of flight hours, steaming days, major ground exercises, and the like (now that the pain of sequestration back in 2013 has been ended, even if the damage from that unfortunate occurrence has not yet been fully repaired).

Some point out that defense spending from 2011 through 2020 has been cut by a cumulative total of about $1 trillion already. That is largely true—not even counting reductions in war-related costs, and even assuming no return to sequestration-level budget caps. The cuts include what Secretary of Defense Robert Gates did during the first two years of the Obama administration with various cancellations and efficiency innovations (though these savings were largely redirected to other defense priorities that had arguably been underfunded previously). Further cuts, including to the actual defense budget topline, occurred after the "Tea Party revolution" of 2010 and the 2011 Budget Control Act. The latter legislation effected a half-trillion dollars in ten-year savings. Additionally, it raised the possibility of yet another tranche of cuts, commonly referred to as sequestration (actually, sequestration being the mechanism by which cuts would be implemented if necessary), of similar combined magnitude. Those sequestration-level provisions of the Budget Control Act have loomed over the Pentagon (and the rest of government) ever since, leading to the temporary imposition of across-the-board reductions in budgets for part of 2013 and threatening to return in whole or in part ever since. Certainly, this final tranche of possible cuts associated with sequestration and all the chicanery that goes with it has been regrettable.

But defense spending did need to go down. All of these cuts have been made relative to a very high annual level of more than $750 billion in national defense budgets over the 2008–11 period. That level easily exceeded the real-dollar peaks of the Reagan buildup, Vietnam War, and Korean War. It was more than we need now, and that late Bush/early Obama period should not be retroactively defined as the gold standard in defense spending or strategy.

As such, while my proposal would rescind sequestration-level cuts and add modestly more to the military budget than intended by President Obama, I do not go so far as the 2014 National Defense Panel Review of the 2014 Quadrennial Defense Review. That panel, led by William Perry and John Abizaid, encouraged a full repudiation of the Budget Control Act of 2011—not only the "sequestration" cuts but the initial reduction of $500 billion over ten years as well.[2] To my mind, that first $500 billion in reductions should be largely acceptable, especially if some key reforms can be accomplished. It is the second tranche of such reductions, to be imposed by sequestration in the absence of other decisions or means, that is problematic and excessive.

Some may understandably ask why U.S. military spending needs to be substantially larger than the Cold-War inflation-adjusted average. Part of the reason is the increased cost of doing business, given trends in the expense of weaponry and in compensation and in operating costs for the Department of Defense. The rest of the reason, in short, is the world today, with its multiple threats, crises, and conflicts.

These circumstances require an engaged and strong United States. American military superiority is a good thing for global stability in general, as well as U.S. and allied interests in particular. While not in jeopardy per se, that superiority is under strain and stress.

American national defense resources are no longer nearly as great by proportion with the budgets of China and Russia as a decade or two ago. U.S. military spending may well be, as President Obama noted in his 2016 State of the Union address, equal to the next eight highest-spending countries combined.[3] But defense budgets do not always dictate combat outcomes, or ensure effective deterrence. Chinese precision missiles, Russian advanced air defenses, and other such assets— whether operated by Beijing and Moscow or sold to other parties—can cause asymmetric, disproportionate effects.[4] New technologies offer promise for America's armed forces, but also new ways for adversaries to challenge or hurt the United States—as such, it is important for the Department of Defense to have enough resources to pursue modernization itself, and respond to real or anticipated innovations by others.

U.S. military spending is indeed large. But it is now only about three to four times that of China, after having been nearly ten times as great at the turn of the century. That may sound like a comfortable advantage. It is not, especially when the correct strategic goal for the United States is not primarily to defeat China in combat but rather to deter combat in the first place, while also operating in many other parts of the world. China, by contrast, has the luxury of being able to concentrate its strategic energies on the western Pacific region alone. And while America's allies are wealthy and numerous in many cases, they have not kept their military spending levels as high as most had promised, and they have not always spent their resources well.

U.S. defense spending as a percent of the economy, as noted, is down to about 3 percent of GDP, after having reached nearly 5 percent in the latter Bush and early Obama years—and after approaching 6 percent under Ronald Reagan and averaging around 8 percent in the latter 1950s and 1960s. That 3 percent figure is much less relative to the size of the economy than was the case even in the days of the "hollow Army" of the post-Vietnam 1970s. Also, today's U.S. military of some 1.3 million active-duty uniformed personnel is much smaller than the Cold-War force that exceeded 2 million during its latter decades. It is also smaller than China's and not much bigger than the Indian or North Korean militaries, by way of comparison. High personnel costs, while appropriate for an all-volunteer force that must be excellent to compensate for its modest size, do sometimes crowd out funds for investment. A decade of national budgetary shenanigans such as sequestration, overlapping with a decade and a half of war, have taken a toll on the American armed forces as well.

Already in recent decades, defense as well as nondefense discretionary spending levels have declined dramatically while entitlements have grown. The nation's annual federal budget deficits are now projected to rise above the trillion-dollar level as soon as 2022, with deficits as a percent of GDP doubling to nearly 5 percent by 2026 and total debt held by the public reaching 86 percent of GDP by 2026, according to CBO projections from January of 2016. But that is not the result of excessive military spending. Some 90 percent of the expected deficit growth is due to entitlements and interest, and defense spending now accounts for only about 15 percent of the federal budget. Military spending must be efficient, to be sure, but it cannot be the nation's piggy bank for other needs or for reestablishing fiscal prudence.[5]

CHAPTER 3

Principles of American Military Strategy and Posture

With these defense basics in mind, if the above logic of preserving the peace, protecting the commons, helping ensure the safety of allies, and discouraging the spread of dangerous technologies like nuclear weapons is the right grand strategy for the United States, how should American armed forces contribute to the effort? Which core strategic pillars of current defense policy should be retained, and which if any should be modified? My main suggestions would preserve most of today's existing strategic logic, but with an important change or two.

CHINA'S RISE, AND THE REBALANCING TOWARD THE ASIA-PACIFIC

One principle that should continue to guide the next American president is an innovation that occurred in the first term of the Obama administration, and that received widespread bipartisan support—the notion of a rebalancing of not only

American military power, but economic and diplomatic emphasis as well, toward the broader Asia-Pacific region.

The case for emphasizing the Asia-Pacific region is powerful. North Korea remains a serious threat, with erratic and bellicose behavior continuing under its new leader, Kim Jong-Un. The country has, as of May 2016, detonated four nuclear weapons and apparently continues to expand its arsenal.

China has established itself as a peer to the United States by many economic and manufacturing measures, if not in all areas of high technology (and certainly not in per capita income or international influence broadly defined). It now has the second largest military budget in the world bar none, and by early in the 2020s could be spending half as much on its armed forces as does America—with far fewer geographic zones of responsibility on which to focus its military. Its capital stocks of advanced combat aircraft, advanced submarines, other naval vessels, and ballistic and cruise missiles have grown enormously; the majority of its main platforms in these categories can probably now be defined as relatively modern, and gradually approaching parity with the United States.[1] Moreover, it is again reducing the overall size of its military, and especially its army, to facilitate such improvements in quality.[2]

Factoring in everything from aircraft carriers to fifth-generation fighters like the F-22 to its newest attack submarines, the United States still has a major lead over the PLA. Its overall capital stock of modern military equipment is worth nearly ten times that of China.[3] But the overwhelming superiority once enjoyed by the United States is largely gone, and it will be difficult if not impossible to recreate, even with catchy slogans like Air-Sea Battle (until recently) and the "third offset" currently guiding its efforts. It is this context, together with other dynamism in the broader area, that gave rise to the Obama administration's emphasis on the Asia-Pacific region.

The military changes associated with the rebalance are not revolutionary, but they are significant—that is, if they are sustained, and if budgetary pressures do not prevent them from being achieved. Former Secretary of Defense Leon Panetta's June 2012 speech at the Shangri-La Security Dialogue in Singapore suggested that in coming years, the Pacific would receive the focus of 60 percent of American maritime assets and the broader Atlantic region only 40 percent. As he put it, "And by 2020 the Navy will reposture its forces from today's roughly 50/50 percent split between the Pacific and the Atlantic to about a 60/40 split between those oceans. That will include six aircraft carriers in this region, a majority of our cruisers, destroyers, Littoral Combat Ships, and submarines."[4] Four Littoral Combat Ships will be based in Singapore, in fact. The Marine Corps will rotate up to 2,500 Marines at a time in Darwin, Australia. More modest but notable shifts are also occurring in Air Force assets in the region. Secretary of Defense Chuck Hagel stated at the 2013 Shangri-La conference that 60 percent of many Air Force assets will also focus on the Asia-Pacific region, though given the nature of Air Force basing, that may be a less consequential change.[5] Missile defenses are being buttressed somewhat, too, with North Korea's threat providing the main impetus.[6]

One needs to be careful in interpreting these changes. In fact, the Pacific Fleet can provide assets to the Persian Gulf, so the 60-40 split does not necessarily mean that 60 percent of U.S. naval assets will deploy exclusively to the Pacific in the years ahead. Air Force assets are even more easily and quickly redeployed than are ships. And in fact, some aspects of the 60-40 Navy apportionment preceded Panetta's speech by several years, dating back to the George W. Bush

administration.[7] But this set of announcements does nonetheless reflect a significant shift.

Of course, it is not just how many ships are in the Pacific,
but how they are used. The Department of Defense's freedom
of navigation activities in the South China Sea, and the earlier public commitment to treat the Senkaku/Diaoyu islands
as being covered by Article V of the U.S.-Japan Security
Treaty, are wise moves (Washington takes no position on the
rightful owner of those islands, but since they are currently
administered by Tokyo, it has agreed that the islands are covered by the treaty). Were China to continue reclaiming and
militarizing islands in the South China Sea, the most logical
next response by Washington could be exploration of closer
security ties with various states in the region (someday perhaps including new bases). In short, the general policy of pa-
tient, quiet firmness is sound. It also requires resources.

AN ARMY—AND A MILITARY—OF "PENTATHLETES"

Another broad principle for American defense planning
is this: after a number of years of cutbacks, and of falling
somewhat out of strategic vogue, the Army should no longer
be reduced in size or in the scope and range of its possible
missions. And that second point is true for the military as a
whole, despite the Obama administration's hopes that stabilization missions and related operations could be relegated
to a much less central role in American defense policy.

After the Army's long, difficult wars in Iraq and Afghanistan, some critics have argued that the entire notion of attempting to prepare America's ground forces for such complex
missions is a fruitless or even counterproductive exercise.
Harking back in some ways to the Army's attitude of the late
1970s and 1980s, when in the aftermath of the Vietnam War

the Army eschewed preparation for counterinsurgency and focused instead on high-end maneuver warfare operations of the type eventually employed in Iraq in both 1991 and 2003, they favor a force with a more limited orientation.[8] Indeed, the 2012 Defense Strategic Guidance relegated large-scale counterinsurgency campaigns or other stability operations to a far less central place in U.S. force planning (somewhat ironically, after Secretary Rumsfeld had done just the opposite and elevated their importance in 2005, despite much of the GOP's traditional aversion to what it called nation building). That 2012 Guidance stated, "U.S. forces will retain and continue to refine the lessons learned, expertise, and specialized capabilities that have been developed over the past ten years of counterinsurgency and stability operations in Iraq and Afghanistan. However, U.S. forces will no longer be sized to conduct large-scale, prolonged stability operations."[9] As the Defense Strategic Guidance makes clear, while this may be an issue first and foremost for the U.S. Army, it actually involves all the services (and indeed, all of government, with especially important roles for the State Department, the Agency for International Development, and the Justice Department—though other agencies such as the Department of Agriculture have a role to play as well).

There are problems with this logic, which was repeated in the 2014 Quadrennial Defense Review. However adamantly leaders in Washington declare their lack of interest in large-scale land operations, and most specifically in stabilization missions, the enemy gets a vote as well. Put differently, to paraphrase the Bolshevik adage, the United States may not have an interest in stabilization missions, but they may have an interest in us.

To depict high-end, decisive-maneuver warfare as the "traditional" U.S. Army or Marine Corps mission, as many do, is to forget the history of American ground forces, which began with an irregular conflict against the British in the Revolutionary War, spent much of the nineteenth century in battles against Native Americans that were far from classic high-end combat, conducted major operations from the Philippines to Cuba and Central America in the late nineteenth and early twentieth centuries, and engaged in complex missions in Vietnam, Iraq, and Afghanistan. More generally, the notion that ground combat between or within states ever was typified by gentlemanly or otherwise highly regularized standards and protocols is inconsistent with much if not most of human history, as Max Boot and others have cogently argued. Guerrilla and irregular warfare are the norm more than the exception. It is true that, especially in World War II, and to a degree World War I and after Vietnam, an ethos of decisive battlefield triumph in "traditional" combat missions permeated much American military thinking.[10] But it was not even a continuous reality from the 1910s through the 1990s, as noted. And when oversimplified thinking about future war did carry the day, the nation often went astray into costly and sometimes bloody blunders.[11]

The comments of General David Petraeus in a speech at his August 2011 retirement ceremony are worth recalling here:

It will be imperative to maintain a force that not only capitalizes on the extraordinary experience and expertise in our ranks today, but also maintains the versatility and flexibility that have been developed over the past decade in particular. Now, please rest assured that I'm not out to give one last boost to the Counterinsurgency Field Manual, or to try to recruit all of you for COINdinista nation. I do believe, however, that we have relearned since 9/11 the timeless lesson that we don't always get to fight the wars for which we are most prepared or most inclined. . . . Given that reality, we will need to maintain the full-spectrum capability that we have developed over this last decade of conflict in Iraq, Afghanistan, and elsewhere.[12]

The Army's 2014 Operating Concept, "Win in a Complex World," reflects a similar perspective, namely, that the current and future Army must be ready to handle a wide range of possible challenges.[13] It accords with Petraeus's view that the modern soldier must in effect be a "pentathlete," with skills across a wide range of domains that apply to many possible types of operations.[14] General Raymond Odierno, Army Chief of Staff from 2011 through 2015, also frequently underscored his view that the "velocity of instability" in the world has increased—even as major land wars in the broader Central Command region have declined in scale. In late 2014, for example, the Army participated in named contingency operations on five continents, all at once. It had seven of its ten division headquarters deployed in support of these operations.[15] Beyond their sheer number, what was also striking was the varied character of these missions.

As noted, the Bush administration, though initially averse to missions that smacked of nation building, came to understand these realities. Its thinking was reflected, among other places, in the DOD's Directive 3000.05, issued in 2005, which stated that "stability operations are a core U.S. military mission . . . . They shall be given priority comparable to combat operations."[16] It was largely in the aftermath of this change in official doctrine that U.S. forces dramatically improved their battlefield performance in the counterinsurgencies of the 2000s, most notably with the Iraq surge of

2007–08. Even though there were many frustrations with the conflicts in Iraq and Afghanistan, the U.S. military achieved one of the great operational comebacks in its history in Iraq in particular, once it truly took counterinsurgency seriously. Moreover, the difficulties encountered in these wars were largely due to strategic mistakes, including poor civilian guidance on how to stabilize Iraq after Saddam Hussein's overthrow; wholesale disbanding of the Iraqi army and an overly sweeping purge of Baathists from future Iraqi political life, which gave many Sunnis incentive to rebel; and inattention to the development of viable state institutions in Afghanistan during the period of relative calm there from 2002 through 2006, which might have left Kabul better positioned to fend off the Taliban itself.

It is important not to conflate the setbacks in these conflicts with some presumed American incapacity to handle insurgencies effectively. As John Nagl has argued persuasively, counterinsurgency has always been akin to "eating soup with a knife," and not just for the U.S. military.[17] Counterinsurgency operations are very difficult, slow, costly, and undesirable when a viable alternative approach is available. But they are not a type of mission beyond the reach of U.S. military competence—and they are sometimes not a type of mission that is easily avoidable on strategic grounds.

In any event, it is important that future administrations retain the counterinsurgency and stabilization skill sets—not only to conduct such missions with U.S. troops, but to be able to advise others on such operations as well.[18] Indeed, as the Clinton, Bush, and Obama administrations have realized, these challenges go well beyond DOD to involve much of government and other actors as well. Many of these other capacities are far from adequate.[19] Thus, it is not enough for DOD to retain, and indeed improve further, its capacities for such operations. As the government agency with by far the most resources, it must remain sufficiently focused on these kinds of missions to play a successful prodding role in ensuring that the entirety of the U.S. government—as well as America's alliances, the UN system, and other actors— improve their capabilities for such operations. We are probably not done with them yet.

All that said, there is no denying that there is some inherent tension between broadening the skill set of the future U.S. trooper and preparing him or her for excellence in core skills. If the peacetime Army becomes fixated on a laundry list of superficial preparations for a range of hypothetical missions, the excellence that has characterized the American army at war could be jeopardized.[20] The U.S. Marine Corps creed of "every Marine a rifleman" constitutes a useful reminder of how to prioritize and sequence the education and training of any trooper.[21] So while preparing for a broad set of tasks, the Army and Marine Corps, in particular, need to retain focus and simplicity—they must not become slaves to regulation or to long checklists of preparation for myriad secondary tasks. A modest number of demanding exercises mimicking stability or counterinsurgency or other complex missions is better than a slew of "certifications" for many minor and secondary tasks.

ALLIES AND PARTNERS

What of America's many allies around the world? What is their role in defense planning?

It is a good thing, not only for those countries but also the United States, that a strong if loosely structured western alliance system exists. At times it risks dragging the United States into conflicts the country might prefer to avoid. Caution and care are needed to avoid such entrapment at times. Washington has been relatively successful at this. While there have been some U.S. allies that have sometimes asserted themselves too much in one way or another—Taiwan in promoting steps towards independence in the 1990s and early 2000s, for example, or Israel in its settlement policies—these examples are fairly few and far between. Moreover, the two cases noted above do *not* involve treaty allies per se, and the United States has in fact deliberately created ambiguity about whether it would come to the direct defense of either, especially should they seem to have a hand in provoking their own conflicts.

Most important interstate wars since World War II—the North Korean invasion of South Korea, various Arab-Israeli wars, the Iran-Iraq War, the Iraqi invasion of Kuwait, Soviet and Chinese attacks on their neighbors at various junctures, the Tanzanian-led overthrow of Idi Amin in Uganda, the Vietnamese-led overthrow of the Khmer Rouge in Cambodia, conflicts in the Horn of Africa—were initiated by countries that were not U.S. allies. An exception has been the Indo-Pakistani wars—but it is hard to blame the United States for these conflicts, given that their genesis predated its role as anyone's ally in South Asia. Those who argue about entrapment seem more worried about the theoretical possibility than concerned with the empirical record to date. On balance, the U.S. alliance system would appear to have been a remarkably powerful stabilizing force in world politics, not only helping win the cold war but also helping produce the most stable period of interstate relations in modern world history.

The nature of allied and coalition help will be a strong function of the specific challenge at hand. Generally, the contributions of most allies will be quite limited. The 2003 Iraq War is a good case in point. Only Britain provided initial invasion forces that were truly significant and proportionate in some way to America's contribution when adjusted for the respective size of the two countries' militaries and populations.

NATO's average military spending level now fails to equal even 1.5 percent of GDP, well below the modest alliance goal of 2 percent. Even traditional stalwarts are often lagging today. Britain, for example, is cutting its active-duty army to less than half the size of the U.S. Marine Corps; even its much-ballyhooed defense budget increase will augment equipment purchases by less than 10 percent over the next decade.[22] For all the talk of an East Asian arms race, most major American security partners there continue to spend modest fractions of their total national wealth on their armed forces—just under 2 percent for Taiwan, 2 percent for Australia, still only 1 percent for Japan, and 2.5 percent for South Korea.[23]

The United States is blessed by having the strongest coalition of security partners in world history, together constituting some 70 percent of world GDP and world military spending. Yet it is also constrained severely by the deep-rooted limitations of what these sixty or so nations are willing to do to provide for broader regional and global security in addition to their own security.

On balance, the future will probably closely resemble the past. Allied troop contributions could range from the 20 to 30 percent that characterized much of the Iraq War (excluding the Iraqi forces themselves) to the levels of 70 percent or more that have typified some prolonged peace implementation missions. It is regrettable, to be sure, that in some operations allies would likely not be able to do more. But the United States must also bear in mind that if the glass is half empty, it is also half full, and the strength of the nation's broader security coalition is among its most important strategic assets. Moreover, that coalition endures largely because it is flexible, and Washington does not generally try to strong-arm other nations into participating in operations they do not find serve their own security interests.

Beyond warfare, the United States will surely wish to continue helping train overseas allies and other partners.[24] Other countries can and do contribute to such training, to be sure.[25] But the excellence of American armed forces, and their widely recognized capability as the world's best, makes the United States the natural leader in such efforts—a role that should not be undervalued in future discussions of the proper size and capacities of the U.S. Army or the other American military services either.

The United States bases or deploys roughly 15 percent of its active-duty strength abroad at any given time. But the costs of U.S. forward presence in places such as Korea and Germany are generally not high relative to other defense expenses. Typical additional annual costs are usually in the low tens of thousands of dollars per person—meaning about $1 billion a year for every 30,000 to 40,000 personnel abroad, roughly—in such situations. (By contrast, in active war zones like Iraq and Afghanistan, costs have been closer to $1 billion for every 1,000 U.S. uniformed personnel, or about $1 million per trooper per year deployed.)[26] Some might still argue against a forward presence on the grounds that it reduces allies' incentives to provide for their own defense. But empirically, the evidence for this claim is unpersuasive. Indeed, NATO allies reduced their military spending considerably, and at a faster pace than the United States, when the United States dramatically downsized its forces in Europe after the Cold War and then cut further in the 2000s.[27] South Korea remains among the most stalwart of American

TABLE 3-1. *U.S. Troops Based in Foreign Countries*[a]

Country or region	Number of troops
EUROPE	
Belgium	1,216
Germany	38,491
Italy	11,354
Portugal	617
Spain	2,170
Turkey	1,518
United Kingdom	9,124
Other	1,282
Subtotal	65,772
FORMER SOVIET UNION	87
EAST ASIA AND PACIFIC	
Japan	49,396
South Korea	24,899
Other	1,360
Subtotal	75,655
NORTH AFRICA, NEAR EAST, AND SOUTH ASIA	
Bahrain	3,373
Qatar	610
Other	1,080
Subtotal	5,063
SUB-SAHARAN AFRICA	388
WESTERN HEMISPHERE	
Cuba (Guantanamo)	732
Other	889
Subtotal	1,621
Subtotal: all foreign countries, not including war deployments	148,586

(continued)

TABLE 3-1. *(continued)*

Country or region	Number of troops
CONTINGENCY OPERATIONS SUPPORT	
Afghanistan	9,800
Kuwait	11,865
Iraq/Syria	3,500
Other/unknown	40,266
Subtotal	65,431
Total currently abroad	214,017

Source: Department of Defense, "DoD Personnel, Workforce Reports & Publications" (www.dmdc.osd.mil/appj/dwp/dwp_reports.jsp). Richard Sisk, "Carter Signals US Plans to Deploy More Troops to Iraq," Military.com, January 25, 2016. David Jolly, "U.S. to Send More Troops to Aid Afghan Forces Pressed by Taliban," *New York Times*, February 8, 2016.

a. Numbers as of February 2015, except early 2016 for Iraq and Afghanistan. Only countries with at least 500 troops are listed individually. These totals do not include U.S. Navy and Marines at sea. Some contingency operation numbers are likely lower in 2016.

allies, spending a considerably higher fraction of its GDP on armed forces than the average, despite a strong ongoing U.S. troop presence on the peninsula. There is no clear correlation in general between the United States doing more and its allies doing less to help themselves, or vice versa.

On balance, the United States has many challenges in its alliance relationships—but it is far better off with those problems, and those allies, than it would be without them.

CHAPTER 4

A Future Military Plan and Posture for the United States

How then to translate these military principles and priorities into an actual budget—complete with forces, weapons modernization plans, and deployment as well as forward presence characteristics?

READINESS

A good place to begin the broad discussion of U.S. defense policy is with the question of readiness. Readiness, to be useful as a planning concept, should be defined somewhat narrowly as the ability of the military to carry out tasks it has been assigned or told to prepare for. The broader question of long-term innovation—and the question about what purposes American armed forces should serve, of "ready for what?"—should be viewed separately. So should matters of force sizing.[1] Viewed in this light, readiness still encompasses a broad range of issues, ranging from the quality and experience levels of military personnel to the serviceability

TABLE 4-1. *DoD Budget and Budget Request by Service, FY 2016 and 2017*

Billions of 2016 dollars[a]	FY 2016 enacted	FY 2017 request
DEPARTMENT OF THE ARMY		
Military personnel	58.2	57.5
Operations and maintenance	60.0	63.3
Procurement	19.4	18.1
RDT&E	7.6	7.6
Military construction	1.1	0.8
Family housing	0.4	0.5
Revolving and management funds	0.2	0.1
Total Army	*146.9*	*148.0*
DEPARTMENT OF THE NAVY		
Military personnel	45.7	46.1
Operations and maintenance	54.5	55.0
Procurement	47.8	44.8
RDT&E	17.9	17.4
Military construction	1.9	1.3
Family housing	0.3	0.4
Revolving and management funds	0.4	—
Total Navy	*168.8*	*164.9*
DEPARTMENT OF THE AIR FORCE		
Military personnel	34.7	35.2
Operations and maintenance	55.3	57.2
Procurement	45.1	43.9
RDT&E	24.5	28.1
Military construction	1.6	1.9
Family housing	0.4	0.3
Revolving and management funds	0.1	0.1
Total Air Force	*161.8*	*166.9*

TABLE 4-1. *(continued)*

DEFENSEWIDE

Military personnel	—	—
Operations and maintenance	74.5	75.3
Procurement	6.5	5.3
RDT&E	19.0	18.7
Military construction	2.2	2.2
Family housing	−0.1	0.1
Revolving and management funds	0.5	1.3
Total Defensewide	*102.8*	*102.9*
Total budget	580.3	582.7

Source: Office of the Under Secretary of Defense (Comptroller) Chief Financial Officer, Defense Budget Overview FY 2017 (Washington, D.C., February 2016), Appendix A, A–7.

a. Figures are based on the president's budget request for 2017. Totals include all war and enacted supplemental funding. Numbers may not add due to rounding.

of their equipment to the adequacy of their training and other preparations.

Defined thusly, U.S. military readiness today is on balance fairly good, at least unit by unit. Start with weaponry. Most equipment is in fairly good shape. For example, Army equipment on average has mission-capable rates today exceeding 90 percent, according to Army officials with whom I have spoken, a historically high level. That said, some types of weapons such as many aircraft are aging fairly substantially— underscoring the need for a procurement plan that emphasizes not only quality but adequate quantity as well.

Training was disrupted by sequestration in recent years and wartime demands before that, but it is recovering. There is a backlog of missed training cycles and other readiness shortfalls that will take time to address fully (even if the next president and Congress avoid the foolishness of a possible return to sequestration and other budgetary brinkmanship and shenanigans).[2] But on balance the situation is much improved now. Take some specific examples: The Army is again resourcing a sustainable level of training with brigade rotations to the national training centers (almost twenty such rotations a year). The Navy is operating at a pace adequate to put crews and ships through major training cycles every two to three years now, depending on ship type. The Marine Corps is putting twelve infantry battalions a year through large training exercises, out of an overall number roughly twice that large in the whole force. And the Air Force is funding various components of its readiness programs at 80 to 98 percent of preferred resource levels.[3] To illustrate the point further, as an example of the fact that today's force remains reasonably well trained, Navy on-duty fatalities have declined from an annual average of about twenty in the 2004–06 period to fewer than ten in the Obama administration.[4]

A third matter, probably the most important, is the question of people. Attracting and retaining high-quality military personnel is clearly crucial to the nation's long-term military preparedness. Today, recruiting and retention statistics are generally good, and today's all-volunteer force is generally highly educated and experienced.[5] Indeed, statistically it is quite good. For example, typical scores of new recruits on the armed forces qualification test have improved considerably over time relative to the population at large. They are now significantly better than in the Reagan years or the immediate pre-9/11 period (two useful benchmarks for comparison). Mean time in service, a reflection of the experience of the force (albeit an imperfect gauge of overall quality), now averages about eighty months in the enlisted ranks. That is not quite as good as in the 1990s when averages were eighty-five to ninety months, but better than the seventy-five-month period that typified the Reagan years or the lower figures of the 1970s.[6] To consider one service, albeit the one least affected by the wars of this century, Navy reenlistment rates have been about 25 percent higher over the last fifteen years than during the Reagan years (and almost twice as high as during the "hollow force" years of the late 1970s); attrition rates of those leaving the service before finishing a planned tour are also at historic lows.[7]

Of course, there are cracks and strains—and no case for complacency when looking into the future. Some of the problems are quite severe; for example, the increases in divorce rates and suicides that occurred during the war years of the recent past. Some of the most severe strain seems to be alleviating. Divorce rates averaged across the services were about 2.7 percent in the year 2000, growing to a peak of about 3.7 percent in 2010/2011 and since declining to about 3.0 percent, for example. But the residual effects of the strain imposed on the force, military personnel, and their families by the wars and other challenges of the twenty-first century still endure.[8] For example, within the Department of the Navy, the suicide rate, while still not higher than the general population, has trended upward, from fewer than ten per 100,000 to about fifteen per 100,000 personnel since 2003.[9]

I would offer several suggestions. If the recruit pool for the military is inadequate, it should be increased through a variety of measures. One means is to get behind the campaign led by General Stanley McChrystal to dramatically increase the prevalence of national service in the country. This would *not* be a draft; no one would serve in the military except voluntarily. But by supporting a national campaign to dramatically increase national service of all types, the military could benefit for its own specific purposes as well. In addition, to the extent that too many young Americans fail to meet fitness standards, how about a ten-week *pre-boot-camp* concept as suggested by New York businessman and philanthropist Marshall Rose that would grant direct access to traditional military boot camp if potential recruits passed the fitness regimens of the precursor course? As for retention, there are also a number of things that should change. Most have to do with the expectations placed on those who wish to stay in the military and keep seeking promotions; they have little flexibility in their allowable career paths today and many with family or personal or professional constraints wind up leaving as a result. A more flexible personnel system that allowed for sabbaticals or even departure and reentry, among other options, could do a great deal to ensure that a wider range of individuals choose to stick with military service. Such ideas remain largely in the conceptual stages in today's military.[10] That should accelerate dramatically in the years ahead.

FROM TWO WARS TO A "1 + 2" FRAMEWORK FOR AN ARMY OF A MILLION SOLDIERS

How to size and posture the U.S. Army for the world ahead? How many wars and other major operations does America's military realistically need to handle at a time? What other missions should be central in its thinking?

These questions are also of relevance to the U.S. Marine Corps, though as a smaller service and a part of the Department of the Navy as well, the Marine Corps has a separate identity and separate rationale for its force structure beyond that of preparing for ground combat. As such, the below discussion focuses on the Army, assuming that the future of the U.S. Marine Corps should be largely one of continuity in terms of force size and structure.

One caveat to that general approach, however, concerns a specific and contentious matter of overseas basing. To the extent the Marine Corps is unable to carry out its intended plans for relocating forces on Okinawa, specifically from the Futenma Air Station to a new offshore facility near Henoko further north on the island, it should consider reducing overall force totals on Okinawa substantially. It could then bring more Marines back to regular stationing in the United States. To compensate strategically, and avoid any lessening of its perceived or actual commitment to the Western Pacific region, it could, with Japanese financial support, increase its pre-positioned supplies there. It could also obtain contingency access to Japanese facilities on the island and in other parts of Japan, as Mike Mochizuki and I have long argued. But this issue is such a moving target that I leave it aside for the main purposes of this paper.[11]

Back to the Army. During the Cold War, the character of plausible threats combined with the existence of a single Communist bloc largely centered on Moscow typically led to some form of two-war capability as the objective for American military capacity. American defense posture varied between periods of major ambition—as with the "2½ war" framework of the 1960s that envisioned simultaneous conflicts against the Soviet Union (probably in Europe), China in East Asia, and some smaller foe elsewhere—and somewhat more realistic approaches. Notably, President Nixon reduced the planning requirement to 1½ wars, while asking more of America's global allies as the principal response force and deterrent, particularly in Asia. Nixon's "1 war" would have been conflict in Europe against the Warsaw Pact; a regional conflict elsewhere provided the basis for his additional "½ war" capability.[12]

These military-planning frameworks grew out of the Cold-War logic of containment, which identified key American strategic interests abroad in western Europe and Japan and eventually the Middle East as well. Since there was believed to be a single central adversarial entity orchestrating trouble around the world, and looking for opportunities to exploit, it was considered especially important that America and its allies have the capacity to respond to more than one specific crisis or conflict at a time.[13]

Throughout the 1990s, U.S. ground forces were sized and shaped primarily to maintain a two-regional-war capability. This was true even though there was no longer a single calculating adversary with global ambition and the capacity to cause multiple, overlapping crises or wars. But the logic of being able to deter a second potential adversary while fighting a first was still considered powerful, especially since the United States wound up facing conflicts or at least severe crises in both Iraq and North Korea within a short period of time in the 1990s.

According to this post–Cold War planning framework, the two possible wars were assumed to begin in fairly rapid succession (though not exactly simultaneously), and then overlap, lasting several months to perhaps a year or two. Three separate administrations—Bush 41, Clinton 42, and Bush 43, and a total of five defense secretaries—Cheney, Aspin, Perry, Cohen, Rumsfeld—endorsed some variant of it. They formalized the logic in the first Bush administration's 1992 "Base Force" concept, the Clinton administration's 1993 "Bottom-Up Review," the first Quadrennial Defense Review (QDR) in 1997, and then Secretary Rumsfeld's own 2001 QDR.[14] In these debates in the dozen years following the Cold War and Desert Storm, most considered simultaneous combat in two places unlikely, but the deterrent logic was still seen as useful. In addition, the two-war construct (even if it eventually proved inadequate for the two wars the

United States did fight, in Iraq and Afghanistan) provided a cushion in case a single war proved more difficult than expected. It also provided a capability for "lesser included cases"—military operations other than war—missions that were generally viewed as much lower priorities than main combat operations, but that were nonetheless recognized as not always avoidable.

In short, the history of all these efforts at determining national strategy and establishing reasonable goals and benchmarks for the nation's armed forces includes many judgment calls. There were no scientifically provable right answers. There probably were at least two clear wrong answers—the lack of preparation for the type of combat waged in Vietnam, and the failure to deter the Korean War. The latter resulted from the nation's general military unpreparedness at the time combined with poor signaling about the importance of the peninsula to the United States—including not only Secretary of State Dean Acheson's infamous early 1950 speech, but the earlier decision to remove American combat forces from South Korea in 1948.[15]

In my judgment, a two-land-war capability is no longer necessary. With the demise of Saddam Hussein's regime, the likelihood of a major overland threat by one crucial Middle Eastern state against another has declined, even if the likelihood of disorder in the region has on balance increased since 2003. Korea remains a significant threat, but South Korea's much greater military preparedness than in the past reduces the pressure on the United States for near-term responsiveness—and for avoiding deterrence failure. Other missions, such as a counteroffensive against Russia after a Russian attack on a Baltic state, or a notional invasion of Iran by the United States over a nuclear crisis, are important enough to plan against, but not at all likely to be conducted.

(Still, enhanced deterrence of a Russian military threat to NATO member states makes sense, given Moscow's provocations of the Baltic states and various efforts to undermine their stability in recent years, and given the dramatic downsizing of U.S. capabilities in Europe over the last quarter century to the point where the United States now has only 30,000 Army troops and no heavy brigades in all of Europe.[16])

Deterrence should be part of an integrated policy towards Moscow. (I also favor an ambitious negotiation initiative that would create a zone of neutral states near Russia, and rule out NATO membership options for countries like Ukraine, in return for verifiable Russian withdrawal from those states and Moscow's commitment to the region's long-term security and neutrality.) The deterrence effort need not be large in scale. Were resulting measures overdone, Putin might be provoked as easily as deterred, given his desire for reestablishing Russian greatness and pride and his general prickliness.[17] Thus, the goal should be to shore up NATO's resolute commitment to its member states' security without creating new drama or an action-reaction cycle with Putin. The current effort under the European Reassurance Initiative and Operation Atlantic Resolve to maintain nearly continuous U.S. presence through exercises, and to sustain modest stocks of equipment (totaling 250 heavy fighting vehicles and other assets) in up to seven eastern NATO countries, seems of the correct general magnitude for the moment.[18] Returning a U.S. heavy brigade to Europe, perhaps to Germany as is currently being considered, also seems reasonable.[19] As such, the Obama administration's plan to request more than $3 billion in the 2017 budget for these purposes is sound. It may appear to be a major increase, as it reflects a quadrupling of the 2016 allocation, but in fact, building infrastructure is expensive, and that total allocation is well under 1 percent of the total defense budget. Larger increases are not warranted or wise at this time. Moving towards a genuine, prompt war-winning capability for an intense fight in Eastern Europe would require a major buildup of logistics capabilities, resilient command and control networks, naval assets quickly deployable to the Baltic Sea, air and missile defense systems, and sheer numbers of American personnel.[20] That seems inconsonant with the threat at present, and as likely to make things worse as to make them better. However, greater participation by other NATO allies in the reassurance/deterrence mission, with sustained military presence in the eastern states of a comparable magnitude to the U.S. level, would also be wise—and make the combined effort a manifestation of alliance solidarity as well as defense capability.

All told, I would propose retaining a variant of a two-war capability for the nation's air and maritime forces, as discussed further below, and having a "1+2" framework for sizing the future American ground forces. It is still quite plausible that, in addition to a Korean conflict, a major crisis or conflict could arise with China or Iran, for example. Because either of these nations would be most likely to pose threats at sea, the missions (and the deterrent capabilities designed to reduce the odds of such scenarios from arising in the first place) should be handled largely by the U.S. Air Force and the U.S. Navy. The Marine Corps, or a modest fraction of the Army, could help provide supporting capabilities in realms such as missile defense or base security, and perhaps some limited offensive operations with ballistic missiles.[21] But they would not be expected to have a lead combat role, at least not by comparison with the classic scenarios that have guided American defense planning (and the two-war paradigm) for decades.

For the Army, under this new proposal, the idea would be to have enough capacity for a single, robust, large-scale operation—that is the "1" in the force-sizing construct. The war might or might not lead to regime change and occupation of enemy territory; as Elbridge Colby has persuasively argued, there are many circumstances, especially in a nuclear-armed world, in which attainment of limited military goals would be the far wiser and more realistic course.[22] But with or without unconditional surrender as an objective, a major war could clearly be very large in scale and in demands on the conventional forces including the Army. That would be true, for example, in Korea, where North Korean nuclear weapons, the proximity of DPRK artillery and rockets near Seoul, and the sheer mass of a million-soldier army of well-indoctrinated North Korean youth could make for a formidable foe. (In addition to robust military planning, I would also favor a new diplomatic strategy that sought to limit the size of North Korea's nuclear forces. It might begin by seeking to cap them, a less ambitious goal than the formal denuclearization demand voiced by the United States and others in the on-again, off-again six-party talks. That cap could be monitored by Chinese and Russian inspectors, and it could be rewarded by a loosening of western sanctions—provided that North Korea also agreed to stop the development, testing, and stockpiling of longer-range missiles and ideally also to eliminate its chemical weapons.)

Simultaneously, the United States should have capacity to carry out two potentially difficult and lengthy, and presumably also multilateral, stabilization or deterrent or response missions. These would be more on the scale of the typical post–Cold War U.S. missions in Somalia, Bosnia, Kosovo, or Afghanistan through 2008 (and after 2014).

Often, the nation has conducted two such mid-sized missions at a time, making that number a reasonable standard for sizing future forces. Future such missions could include a U.S. role in a UN peacekeeping or disaster response mission in Congo, Sudan, or Nigeria; an American role in backstopping a multilateral force to implement an Israeli-Palestinian peace accord; an American reassurance and deterrence mission with ground forces in Gulf Cooperation Council (GCC) states in the aftermath of an air strike campaign against Iran's nuclear facilities; or certain hypothetical missions such as peacekeeping and relief in Syria or South Asia.

These ideas ratchet back modestly the warfighting requirements on the U.S. Army. They do not amount to a case for cutting it further in size, however. Indeed, collectively they persuade me that on balance the Army is at the lower end of the reasonable range of where its force structure and end strength should be. Today the Pentagon envisions an active-duty force of some 450,000 soldiers with a combined Reserve and National Guard of about 525,000. In fact, I would argue for a modest increase, to a total Army of 1 million.[23] As the 2016 Commission on the Future of the Army concluded, the Army has an inadequate number of combat aviation assets when measured against war plans and recent patterns of usage, and also a dearth of short-range air defense assets in the active-duty force. While the Army often should make greater use of its reserve component in actual deployments, the commission found there is nonetheless a need for some air-defense capability readily available and deployable in the active force. There is also a strong desirability of permanent stationing of combat aviation assets in Korea. Addressing these shortfalls alone might push the full size of the Army closer to 1 million soldiers.[24]

THE NAVY

Today's U.S. Navy, as with fleets of recent decades, is sized with two purposes in mind. One of course is to win wars if and when they occur; this is always the bedrock consideration for U.S. military planning and is necessary for robust deterrence as well. But second, especially for the Navy—and related to the task of deterrence—is the ability to sustain a significant presence with combat-capable ships in key theaters around the world continuously, with the ability to increase capacity in a crisis. Those key theaters today include, prominently, the broader Persian Gulf region and the western Pacific Ocean. But they also include the Mediterranean Sea, the Baltic Sea, the North Atlantic, and certain other waters. Because major U.S. Navy bases are far away from these theaters, and because crews and ships cannot be sustained on deployment indefinitely, the Navy needs a rotation base to keep up the presence mission. Indeed, any one ship and crew can typically only be on station about one-fourth to one-fifth of the time given current operational practices (that is, perhaps five months out of a twenty-four month ship/crew cycle).

The Navy wishes to enlarge its fleet modestly in coming years. The purpose is partly to give backbone to the notion of the Asia-Pacific rebalance. To wit, while its aggregate "lead" over China in raw tonnage remains large, by a factor of more than two to one, that lead has been shrinking.[25] Perhaps even more importantly, modest growth in the fleet is needed to reduce strains that come from maintaining the current pace of deployments with the current number of ships. For example, while the Navy has reduced its size by roughly 20 percent this century in number of ships, the average number of vessels deployed has remained steady at roughly 100 at any given time.[26] Even if some of those ships are close to home, on less strenuous deployments, and even if some are home-ported abroad, improving the efficiency of their deployments, this is a breakneck pace for a fleet of just 280 ships. Average deployment time for a ship putting to sea on a major deployment has grown from about 150 days in the 2004–06 period to more than 200 days throughout the Obama presidency.[27] Moreover, there have been some notable gaps in fleet presence in key regions, most importantly an inability to sustain an aircraft carrier battle group continuously near the Persian Gulf that manifested itself in latter 2015, and a reduced capacity to surge carriers in any crisis. While the Navy, to my mind, sometimes exaggerates the importance of continuous forward presence—for example, it was excessive to insist on having two carrier battle groups near the Gulf at all times—it is true that in a tense environment such as today's, maintaining a single carrier group near the Gulf at all times would be desirable.[28]

Some question the survivability of the aircraft carrier in the twenty-first century, and wonder why that type of ship should remain the centerpiece in many ways of the U.S. Navy's current and future planned fleet. They are right to ask the question. The carrier is indeed becoming somewhat more vulnerable on balance. But the case for the carrier remains strong nonetheless, for several reasons. First, carriers are still survivable against the vast majority of other countries' militaries if operated a reasonable distance off the shore—as they generally are. Second, even if they could be struck in some cases, it would be a hugely fraught decision by any country to attack an American vessel—not an easy decision for anyone at any time. Even if one or two could be disabled or sunk, moreover, most of the fleet would likely be far enough away from the theater of hostilities that, together with other instruments of U.S. military power, it could mount a very significant counterattack (or use force asymmetrically against the interests of the aggressor in some other theater). In this sense, the carriers that might have been lost would have served a very useful purpose as a demonstration of American commitment, and in effect as a tripwire. Third, it is not obvious that carriers will in fact become fundamentally vulnerable. They have surely become at least somewhat *more* vulnerable than they have been since 1990. But the competition between the carrier and its various nemeses is not over by any means. The United States retains various means to try to sustain carrier survivability as well, including interfering with the reconnaissance and guidance networks of enemies trying to target the carrier—and perhaps someday also having new means of self-defense for its fleet, such as better laser or directed-energy missile defense systems. Trends in technology should indeed lead the United States to continually ask if its investment in aircraft carriers, and surface ships more broadly, should be reduced at least modestly in the decades to come. But the case is not compelling today.

For these and other reasons, the Navy's plan as spelled out in the Fiscal Year 2016 Shipbuilding Plan to increase fleet size to 308 ships is generally reasonable, though perhaps somewhat excessive. [29] Those 308 ships would include eleven aircraft carriers and ten aircraft carrier wings of planes, twelve ballistic-missile submarines, forty-eight attack submarines, eighty-eight major surface combatants, fifty-two smaller surface combatants and mine warfare ships, thirty-three amphibious ships (for the Marine Corps primarily; nine of them at present are in effect small carriers, each carrying up to 20 to 24 aircraft of various types), and sixty-two logistics and support ships.[30] Over time, I believe there are ways to reduce these requirements modestly, using means explained below. As such, I would favor a target closer to 300 ships rather than 308.

The overall trend towards growing the fleet in the Obama years has been good, with the number of ships authorized roughly double what it had been during the Bush years; that fact will indeed permit a near-term growth in the size of the fleet.[31] But more recently, it is struggling to buy the ships needed to sustain the progress. The Navy has scaled back major ship construction in both 2016 and 2017 to seven new starts a year (implying a fleet size of well under 300 ships if sustained). The problem does not stop there. The Congressional Budget Office, noting that new classes of ships typically cost at least 25 percent more than originally intended, estimates that the Navy is underestimating the likely costs of shipbuilding in coming years by roughly $2 billion a year or 10 percent.[32] That is not a herculean problem to surmount, but it is a real problem, and the historical data is overwhelmingly on CBO's side of the debate. The Navy will need to increase shipbuilding budgets, reduce scheduled ship construction, or both. Indeed, since the official plan was released, Secretary of Defense Ashton Carter has curtailed the program for the Littoral Combat Ship (LCS) by twelve ships over the lifetime of the program (and the FY 2017 budget has scaled back shipbuilding somewhat, too, delaying the plan to increase the fleet's size). Whatever one thinks of that LCS ship, it is very affordable relative to almost anything else the Navy buys (at least among major ships that count towards the official fleet size). As such, to the extent that a goal of more than 300 ships remains a real goal, the Navy may need to find $1 billion or more per year to buy more expensive ships to compensate for the reduced purchases of the LCS. In other words, it may face something more like a $3 billion annual shortfall.

TABLE 4-2. *Major Department of Defense Acquisition Programs*

Billions of 2016 dollars		FY 2016		FY 2017	
		Qty	$	Qty	$
AIRCRAFT					
F-35	Joint Strike Fighter	68	11.6	63	10.5
KC-46A	Tanker	12	3.0	15	3.3
P-8A	Poseidon Aircraft	17	3.4	11	2.2
V-22	Osprey Aircraft	20	1.6	16	1.5
E-2D AHE	Advanced Hawkeye	5	1.2	6	1.4
AH-64E	Apache Helicopter	64	1.4	52	1.1
C/HC/MC-130J	Hercules Aircraft	29	2.4	14	1.3
UH-60	Black Hawk Helicopter	107	1.8	36	1.0
CH-53K	King Stallion Helicopter	—	0.6	2	0.8
MQ-4C	Triton UAV	4	1.0	2	0.8
H-1 Upgrades	Bell Helicopter	29	0.9	24	0.8
NGJ	Next Generation Jammer Increment 1[a]	—	0.4	—	0.6
CH-47F	Chinook Helicopter	39	1.1	22	0.7

MISSILE DEFENSE/MISSILES

BMDS	Ballistic Missile Defense	—	7.7	—	6.9
Trident II	Trident II Missile Mods	—	1.2	—	1.2
AMRAAM	Adv. Medium Range Air-Air Missile	429	0.7	419	0.7
SHIPS					
SSN 774	VIRGINIA Submarine	2	5.7	2	5.3
DDG 51	AEGIS Destroyer	2	4.4	2	3.5
CVN 78	FORD Aircraft Carrier	—	2.8	—	2.8
ORR	Ohio Replacement	—	1.4	—	1.9
LHA-6	Amphibious Assault Ship	—	0.5	1	1.6
LCS	Littoral Combat Ship	3	1.8	2	1.6
SPACE					
AEHF	AEHF Satellite	—	0.6	—	0.9
EELV	EELV Launch Vehicle	4	1.5	5	1.8
TRUCKS					
JLTV	Joint Light Tactical Vehicle	804	0.4	2,020	0.7

Source: Office of the Under Secretary of Defense (Comptroller) Chief Financial Officer, Defense Budget Overview FY 2017 (Washington, D.C., February 2016), p. 5-2.

a. Includes base and OCO funding. UAV = unmanned aerial vehicle.

I have three major suggestions for scaling back modestly the Navy's ambitions for a larger fleet. One pertains primarily to the operations of main surface combatants, one to nuclear-armed submarines, and one to the specific security situation in the Persian Gulf.

Consider first main surface combatants. Over the long term, rather than increase its fleet, the Navy could employ innovative approaches like "sea swap," by which some crews are rotated via airplane while ships stay forward-deployed longer than is currently the norm. This can increase the deployable "efficiency" of a ship by roughly a third, for those classes of ships for which it is a practicable concept. It is of greatest relevance to the operations of the Navy's main surface fleet—the 140 or so ships not including aircraft carriers, submarines, or amphibious vessels. In principle, with sea swap, a fleet of 100 to 120 ships (depending on specifics) using the sea swap concept could maintain the same presence as the 140-ship fleet using current methods. More realistically, in the short term the Navy will do well to reduce its requirements by 10 ships with this approach, because it takes time to secure the necessary overseas port access—and also because warfighting needs do not allow for as large a reduction in the fleet as would a simple, narrow focus on the normal presence mission.

As for ballistic missile submarines, to my mind, the Ohio-class replacement vessel need not be thoroughly modernized in every sense of the word. A ship now headed for costing $6 billion a copy on average might be brought down closer to $5 billion, given that the quietness and other main attributes of the Ohio class submarines remain excellent and generally adequate for the job. [33] Moreover, there is a good case for buying only eight such submarines, rather than the twelve now planned, and to the extent necessary relying more on the bomber fleet to maintain overall strategic warhead counts, as I argue further below. The United States would still have a robust triad, insuring among other things against the remote possibility that nuclear-armed ballistic-missile submarines (SSBNs) themselves might become vulnerable over time (perhaps to torpedoes launched from unmanned underwater vehicles that loitered or lay dormant near ports—a point offered to me by Steven Pifer). There would be degradation in the ability to execute the so-called Single Integrated Operational Plan (or SIOP) on short notice with a smaller SSBN fleet. But that SIOP, I would maintain, is a relic of the Cold War, and an undesirable one at that. Survivable forces matter. The capacity for prompt overwhelming response with as many as a thousand or more warheads does not.

That said, it is possible that any savings from a smaller SSBN fleet will be needed to fund a modest expansion of the nuclear-powered attack submarine (SSN) fleet. According to Chief of Naval Operations Admiral John Richardson, today's recommended fleet size was calculated based on a 2006 construct that did not account for the subsequent advances in China's navy or the more assertive global behavior by Russia.[34] As such, while details are murky given the highly classified nature of submarine operations, it is reasonable to assume that the SSN fleet might usefully grow by two to five vessels. Some would argue for substantially larger increases, in fact, based on what combatant commanders are currently requesting.[35] On balance, I do not assume savings in fleet size or cost from this change to SSBN modernization plans. So the alternative fleet size would be about 300 ships, down from 308, based on the sea-swap efficiencies discussed above rather than a cut in subs.

One more idea should be pursued, though it would take time to develop and implement, and as such would not permit a further reduction in fleet size below 300 ships in the near term. It would require considerable cooperation with allies, one of the reasons that pursuing it would take some time. At present the United States relies almost exclusively on aircraft carriers, each carrying about seventy-two aircraft, to have short-range jets in position for possible conflict with Iran in particular. Over the past decade, land-based combat jets formerly based in Saudi Arabia, Kuwait, and Iraq have largely come home. While the United States occasionally rotates fighter jets through the small states of the Gulf Cooperation Council, and while it maintains command and control and support assets in states like Qatar and the UAE, permanent ashore combat power is very limited.

By seeking two or more places to station Air Force combat jets continuously in Gulf states, the United States could ultimately facilitate a reduction in its aircraft carrier fleet, and/or a reemphasis in where the fleet was most commonly deployed. It could permanently end the effort to sustain two aircraft carrier battle groups near the Persian Gulf continuously; indeed, once the idea was well enough developed, it might well be acceptable to have occasional periods when no carriers were nearby. This approach could also liberate remaining carriers to carry out other tasks—and to spend a bit more time in homeport, given the excessive demands of recent schedules. For example, carrier presence could be increased in other demanding regions, such as the South China Sea. (In the Mediterranean Sea, I do not believe that more carrier presence is needed. Here, since there is no true peer rival challenging U.S. interests, large-deck amphibious ships could be employed instead of flat-deck giant aircraft carriers. The amphibious ships cost about $3 billion apiece. Their typical complement of about twenty to twenty-four aircraft per vessel, only a third the number on the larger carriers, should often be adequate for the needs of that region—especially in light of the enormous cost growth in the Ford-class large-deck aircraft carrier, now expected to cost $11 billion to $13 billion a vessel.[36])

Again, this plan and the other efficiencies discussed here should not lead to big cuts in the Navy, however. Reducing the Navy's goal for growing its fleet from the current objective of 308 ships to 300 makes sense. For each possible efficiency that can be imagined, there could be setbacks in American access abroad, or other changing circumstances, that argue for more ships. An Arctic region that is increasingly navigable, and increasingly visited by Russian ships, probably needs more American Navy and Coast Guard attention—implying a need for more than the one operational heavy icebreaker currently available, for example.[37] Also, if turmoil in Egypt ever leads to problems in accessing the Suez Canal, the Navy will need to reach the Persian Gulf only via the Indian Ocean, implying much longer transits than is often the case today with ships going from the North Atlantic to the Mediterranean to the Red Sea and Gulf of Aden. Such a contingency may not be likely, but it is indeed a contingency. As such, while in principle it could be argued that this change in Gulf basing could facilitate a reduction in the carrier fleet by three to four ships, I would favor an eventual reduction of no more than one to two carrier battle groups with this approach.

There is another consideration to keep in mind. On the technology front, more innovation is needed. In some cases this will not lead to a greater demand for ships that count formally against fleet size, but other technologies. In addition to long-range unmanned aircraft to be used for offensive bombing operations and also reconnaissance and fleet air defense, this can include a number of other technologies. Directed energy and certain other forms of advanced missile

defense should be part of the mix. So should robotic underwater vessels operating from a mother ship, unmanned surface vessels providing an outer defense for large vessels
against small-ship threats, and other systems. As such, some
of the efficiencies offered above should be viewed less as
ways to cut the Navy budget and more as ways to free up
resources for entrepreneurial ideas as well as responses to
possible future threat conditions.[38]

TACTICAL COMBAT AIRCRAFT

My recommendations for American airpower resources
focus on the way in which they are being modernized. Their
size strikes me as appropriate. They have been sized for a
quarter century largely for the "2 MRC" or "2 MTW"
mission—that is, being able to conduct and win two overlapping wars known as major regional contingencies or major
theater wars. Although I believe that a less stringent warfighting standard is now adequate for the nation's ground forces,
given the demise of Saddam Hussein and the changing nature of Middle East threats in particular, the earlier standard
is appropriate for American airpower in light of the kinds of
challenges Iran and North Korea, as well as Russia and China,
could possibly pose. Most of these challenges are much more
likely to involve maritime domains than invasions.

The U.S. tactical aircraft modernization agenda centers
on the Lightning II, also known as the F-35 or the Joint
Strike Fighter. All together, the Air Force, Navy, and Marine
Corps still plan to buy nearly 2,500 F-35 combat jets at a
total acquisition price approximating $350 billion in con-
stant 2016 dollars. Almost three-fourths of the funds are yet
to be spent. According to President Obama's 2017 budget
request, the Department of Defense would like to buy

sixty-three of the aircraft in 2017 at a combined price of $10.1 billion, and a total of 404 over the next five years.[39] The Pentagon's independent cost assessment office and CBO have argued in the past that average unit procurement prices could be 15 to 20 percent higher than official estimates. And once purchased, the same Pentagon office estimates that the F-35 will also cost a third more to operate in real terms than planes like the F-16 and F-18 that it is replacing.[40]

It is important to acknowledge numerous strengths of the F-35. It is indeed a stealthy aircraft in a world of improving air defenses, especially those based on the ground. The United States has fought many adversaries since the Cold War ended, but in military terms, they have been quite consistently notable for their lack of sophisticated air defenses. Combat against the likes of Iraq, Serbia, the Taliban in Afghanistan, Libya, and ISIL in Syria and Iraq should not lure us into a false sense of complacency or impunity. Indeed, even on that list of post–Cold War adversaries, Iraq and Serbia caused the United States considerable concern about the safety of its aircraft, and imposed significant burdens and limitations on the nature of aerial operations in a number of missions. For example, extensive preparations against ground defenses were often conducted by aircraft prior to other aerial missions. Altitude limitations were also placed on many planes so they would not be shot down by shoulder-launched man-portable air defenses. With the prospect of more capable foes in the future, some degree of stealth is needed in a large fraction of the nation's ground-attack airpower.

Some have opposed the Marine Corps variant of the plane, with its extra engine as needed for short or vertical take offs and landings. But in fact, that variant has value for an era in which airfields are increasingly vulnerable to precision ordnance of the types that countries such as Iran and

China are fielding. The United States needs enough F-35Bs, as the Marine variant is known, to be able to populate some bases nearest potential combat zones, such as the Gulf states (for scenarios involving Iran) and Okinawa (in regard to China). As former Marine Corps Commandant General James Amos has noted, there are ten times as many 3,000 foot runways in the world adequate for such short-takeoff jets as there are 8,000 foot runways suitable for conventional aircraft—and the Marines can lay down an expeditionary 3,000 foot runway in a matter of days in other places.[41]

Taking all these ideas into consideration, it is important at least to have a "one-war F-35 capability, including some F-35Bs." The United States need not replace every F-16, Harrier Jet, or A-10 with an F-35; refurbishment (or new production of older types of planes) is a good option for per-haps half the aerial fleet. But the nation must be ready for a high-end war even against China, primarily as a means of ensuring deterrence. This requires having enough stealthy aircraft to deploy to most of the carriers and land bases that would be used, for example, in a South China Sea scenario.

Thus, an alternative concept for F-35 production could be as follows. Purchase a total of 1,250 instead of nearly 2,500. Leave the Marine Corps plan largely as is, scaling back only by 10 to 20 percent to account for the proven ca-pacity of unmanned aerial vehicles (UAVs) to carry out some missions previously handled by manned aircraft. Cancel the Navy variant, with its relatively limited range compared with likely needs—buying more F/A-18 E/F Super Hornets in the meantime while committing more firmly to devel-opment of a longer-range unmanned carrier-capable attack aircraft.[42] The United States would still have stealthy bomb-ers and F-35A and F-35B and F-22s, stealthy aircraft, provid-ing a range of low-observable options in virtually any imaginable scenario. The Navy's X-47B unmanned system is also progressing and should be pursued vigorously.[43] Finally, as part of the new approach, reduce planned Air Force purchases, currently expected to exceed 1,700 F-35 planes, by almost half.

Of the 800 planes that the Air Force was counting on, but will not get from the F-35 program under this approach, make up the difference in the following ways. First, retain the A-10 "Warthog" fleet into the future. The Warthog is a proven workhorse for close-air support and is highly relevant to the majority of conflicts that the United States has been fighting—and seems likely to undertake in the future. The Air Force argument that doing so would increase costs seems to forget that the A-10 is already in the inventory and the F-35 is still being purchased. A fair comparison would underscore that the A-10 in fact would save a great deal of money, since whatever refurbishments prove necessary in the future will be far less costly than purchasing F-35 jets. Second, employ further purchases of F-16 jets and refurbishments of existing F-16s to sustain several wings of that type of aircraft.[44] Third, rely more on unmanned aircraft as an integral part of the tactical combat fleet rather than as an add-on. Specifically, the United States can employ the 200 large combat-capable UAVs currently owned by the Air Force, together with the 300 or more on the way, as viable replacements for some manned fighter planes. The Air Force is buying the equivalent of five wings of large UAVs; certainly, it could transform two manned combat wings into unmanned combat aircraft wings as a result.[45]

This approach will produce net savings of some $60 billion in aircraft purchase costs. The F-16 option is still available, but it may not remain available for more than a couple of years, so this option could have to be exercised fairly promptly to make economic sense.[46] Average annual savings from this alternative approach to F-35 production could approach $5 billion, though probably only $2 billion annually in the short term. Over time up to another $2 billion a year or so in savings would be achievable in operating accounts from the sum total of all these changes in tactical aircraft. As noted, the larger savings will not kick in right away, since it is important to get the F-35 production line working efficiently to keep unit costs in check. More of the savings will accrue in the 2020s.

It is true that a certain amount of risk is associated with this alternative plan, since entirely canceling the F-35C Navy version of the plane will leave the Navy with less stealthy aircraft over the next decade. This is a risk, and probably a tolerable one, but not a trivial one. Thus, the Navy does need to keep moving forward with a longer-range unmanned attack aircraft that can operate from aircraft carriers.[47]

THE NUCLEAR WEAPONS MISSION

The United States retains a very large nuclear weapons capability and infrastructure. It encompasses nuclear-armed submarines, land-based missiles, the bomber force, and a number of shorter-range platforms such as tactical combat aircraft capable of delivering nuclear weapons. It also includes a large Department of Energy system responsible for the warheads themselves, not to mention the multi-billion dollar annual cleanup effort to deal with the legacy of the Cold-War nuclear buildup. The costs of all of this are expected to rise considerably in the years ahead, with the annual budget of perhaps $35 billion or so growing by $10 billion and remaining at that higher level for decades, given the current plan to replace today's triad of nuclear delivery vehicles and make other modernizations at DoD and DoE (including deployment of interoperable warheads, based on existing technology, with the first to be called the IW-1).[48] How to pay for this effort—whether through a dedicated DoD-wide fund or traditional service budgets—is controversial at present.[49] That is as it should be, because the price tag is so high. It is too high, in fact.

A large, reliable, safe, flexible American nuclear deterrent is surely necessary. President Obama's vision, articulated in Prague in 2009, of a world free of nuclear weapons at some point in the foreseeable (if distant) future seems even further away than when he first advocated it. The Global Zero movement which had originally hoped for serious multilateral negotiations on eliminating all nuclear weapons from the planet in the course of the 2020s, with a possible realization of that goal in the 2030s, no longer has much momentum. Vladimir Putin more than anyone else has seen to that, though the vision was probably unrealistic from the start, as I have argued elsewhere. A world free of nuclear weapons should remain the ultimate goal. But the pursuit of that goal cannot get too far ahead of the evolution in world politics and the further stabilization of great-power relations that in my mind is a necessary prerequisite to any serious pursuit of the nuclear zero objective.[50]

That said, the United States remains in a somewhat oxymoronic position on the nuclear front. This is perhaps no huge surprise. More than any other domain in the history of American defense policy, nuclear policy has been surreal for decades. This was not all, or even primarily, America's fault. The Cold War with the Soviet Union created huge dilemmas for U.S. national security policy. But a military posture that included the capacity to kill many hundreds of millions of people, while keeping thousands of nuclear weapons on hair-trigger alert as if this was a safe or sustainable practice, was extremely regrettable. Near-misses were more common than many remember in viewing the supposedly stable Cold War through nostalgic, rose-colored glasses. The potential for things to be even more dangerous in the future, in a world of nuclear-armed rival states like India and Pakistan not enjoying a geographic buffer of thousands of miles, and a world in which cyberattacks on nuclear infrastructure can be added to the list of possible dangers to nuclear stability, is foreboding. This is especially true to the extent that newer nuclear powers retain or mimic the counterforce and pre-emptive options of the Cold-War superpowers.[51]

Indeed, vestiges of that policy, and that way of thinking, remain in American strategic policy today. Even though U.S. strategic nuclear forces have declined severalfold since the fall of the Berlin Wall, the United States and Russia each have more than 1,500 strategic nuclear warheads, many of which are on high alert and quickly usable. These numbers contrast with the maximum credible number of warheads that could be militarily useful and consistent with any hope of sustaining civilization on the planet. I would estimate that latter number to be in the dozens or at most low hundreds, depending on the choice of targets (even if weapons of quite moderate yield are introduced into the arsenal, something that could likely be done without testing, incidentally).[52]

Indeed in 2013, the U.S. government concluded that de-ployed U.S. strategic warheads could be reduced another one-third. But that was before Ukraine and Syria. Alas it will be difficult to make further major cuts in U.S. warhead counts as long as President Putin rules Russia. Putin, who has en-gaged in loose talk about nuclear weapons at times, cannot be allowed to think that Russia has become the world's preeminent nuclear power, and he shows no interest in further nuclear arms control. As such, sustaining nuclear parity with Russia remains essential. So does retaining a safe and reliable nuclear force that is entrusted to individuals of the highest standards and training levels; their mission is far too dangerous to be left to anyone else. De-alerting concepts, even unilateral ones, can and should be pursued, but the size of the overall force probably cannot be easily scaled back in the short term.

Still, several ideas in current American nuclear weapons policy are outdated. For example, the Navy continues to argue that the replacement of the Ohio-class ballistic missile submarine with a successor program is its top priority.[53] This does not really make sense, as discussed previously. To be sure, the safety, survivability, and dependability of the sea-based leg of the triad are crucial. But beyond ensuring those goals, the importance of modernization is less compelling. The Navy's logic seems to presume that the Single Integrated Operational Plan (SIOP), now known as OPPLAN 8010, might actually need to be executed at some future date, with most of the strategic force employed in a massive strike. That is not only strategically unwise, but to my mind even unethical as a way of planning American military forces.

A more modest nuclear program could sustain 1,500 strategic warheads and a roughly comparable number of shorter-range systems until Russia is ready to negotiate further cuts (and other powers are ready to think about at least freezing their capabilities). This approach, however, would deemphasize—or even deliberately challenge—the concept of the SIOP with its continued emphasis on nuclear counterforce attacks. It would prioritize safety and reliability above all else, with the retention of some flexibility in how several dozen or at most a few hundred warheads might be employed.

Survivability against a notional enemy first strike would also be emphasized through retention of a nuclear triad, though the details of exactly which capabilities could survive a hypothetical all-out enemy attack would be emphasized somewhat less than in the past. This approach could allow the following changes:

- Reduction in the intended fleet of new ballistic missile submarines from the current total of fourteen Ohio-class vessels, and planned future fleet of twelve new submarines intended to support a complex war plan like today's, to eight vessels. That would still provide the capacity for one vessel, if not two at times, to be deployed continuously in each ocean. (It is also worth noting that if the existing requirement for immediate nuclear response were eliminated, any submarine at sea would achieve the sole remaining goal of high survivability, further easing demands on the fleet.) It would allow commensurate reduction in planned purchases of submarine-launched ballistic missiles when it becomes necessary to replace the D5;

- To the extent possible, a modest reduction in the intended complexity of those submarines, which are presently expected to cost at least $6 billion apiece, more than twice the real cost of the Ohio boats. Even if that $6 billion figure proves difficult to reduce, it should not be allowed to grow significantly;

- Reduction in the planned ICBM force from 400 to 250, and a commitment to long-term reliance on the Minuteman force well beyond 2030 (through additional service-life extension program work on the current force). No new ICBMs would likely be needed, and even if it someday were needed, the date could be delayed, reducing the current bow wave of planned nuclear modernization in the 2020s[54];

■ Either an increase in the warhead loading on the typical D5 missile, or an increase in the number of bombers designated for nuclear use to ensure that the United States retains strategic parity with Russia. Since the United States has many more bombers than it needs for the nuclear mission today, this is primarily a matter of making modest hardware adjustments and keeping a larger number of existing planes and pilots nuclear-certified (on top of their conventional missions); no additional purchases of bombers, beyond those already planned with the Long-Range Strike Bomber program, would be needed;

■ Cancellation of the planned advanced air-launched cruise missile, the Long-Range Stand-Off Weapon, especially in light of the planned acquisition of the stealthy B-21 Long-Range Strike Bomber[55];

■ Reorientation of the Lawrence Livermore National Laboratories away from the nuclear weapons design mission; Livermore would retain some limited capacity as a second repository of expertise on the bomb, but with this concept, the notion of needing two full-fledged independent design laboratories would be changed (Los Alamos being the other).

Savings from this full range of changes would be considerable over the next two decades or so. The scaling back of submarine programs would save at least $24 billion in ships and eventually about $5 billion in missile costs, since fewer D5 missiles would need to be replaced once they reached their expected lifetimes—for an annual average savings of at least $2 billion once operating costs are also factored in. However, as noted before, the savings might be needed to expand modestly the SSN fleet, so no additional net savings are assumed from this change. But other savings are possible too, starting with a reduction of the ICBM force that would save about $500 million annually. Avoiding the need to replace or refurbish those 150 ICBMs that were retired could save close to $1 billion annually (over the longer term, scaling back or even cancelling concepts for a follow-on ICBM could save some considerable fraction of the $62 billion price tag now envisioned for that project—which would imply additional savings of several billion dollars a year).[56]

Cancellation of the cruise missile could save $15 billion to $30 billion, with a best guess in the middle range that would average $1 billion annually. Changes in the DoE nuclear infrastructure, specifically at Livermore, would save another half billion a year—at least enough to balance out the added costs for the bomber force that would come from expanding its role in the nuclear mission (though again, the changes to the bomber force would be intended mainly to sustain parity with Russia, and not to serve as a likely warfighting capability). All told, this more modest amount to nuclear deterrence—emphasizing safety, reliability, and survivability, while retaining full flexibility for a range of modest-scale deterrence missions—would save roughly $3 billion a year.[57]

A final word here is in order on America's possible use of missiles for conventional warfighting purposes, and particularly for theater warfighting purposes. Since the U.S.-Soviet Intermediate-Range Nuclear Forces (INF) Treaty of 1987, the United States has been prohibited (like Russia) from fielding ballistic and cruise missiles with ranges anywhere between 500 and 5,500 kilometers, as a result of nuclear arms control arrangements. But there are reasons to think Russia is not complying with this accord, and obviously China, which was never party to it, is not. There is no need for nuclear-armed missiles of this range. The United States may not require this class of conventional weapon at present, either. However, for some scenarios in the future—ranging from full Russian breakout from the INF Treaty, to an intensifying competition with China in the western Pacific (in which for example the United States felt the need to garrison numerous islands in the Philippines with various offensive capabilities that could threaten China's use of the sea lines)—such a conventional option might become useful and appropriate.

MISSILE DEFENSE

Missile defense remains a major and expensive arena of American military modernization, to the tune of about $9 billion a year in the proposed 2017 budget and closer to $10 billion in 2016. I favor keeping it at roughly current levels—but given its importance, and given the frequent calls by boosters as well as critics that its scale should be considerably increased or reduced, it is worth spelling out the argument.

Through the Obama presidency, missile defense budgets have remained at real-dollar levels comparable to those of Ronald Reagan's Strategic Defense Initiative—even if the goal of Reagan's SDI to render nuclear weapons "impotent and obsolete" remains out of reach, as it almost surely will continue to be in the future. But missile defense can still have important roles, especially in complicating the attack plans of smaller nuclear weapons powers and also in combating conventionally armed ballistic as well as cruise missiles (ballistic missiles are powered only in their launch and boost phases; cruise missiles are essentially unmanned aircraft that are powered throughout flight).

Consider some scenarios where missile defense could be helpful, even if it were far from airtight or perfect in performance. For example, if North Korea someday attained the ability to deliver nuclear weapons intercontinentally, with warheads capable of surviving the flight and missiles capable of delivering warheads many thousands of miles, it could threaten American cities. That in turn could weaken deterrence in a crisis, if North Korea felt it could persuade Washington to back down from resolute behavior. It could also lead U.S. regional allies like South Korea and Japan to doubt America's commitment to their defense (even if that view was unwarranted), possibly persuading them to pursue their own nuclear weapons, and thereby further intensify negative regional security dynamics. But long-range missiles are large, complex, and expensive. So even if North Korea could reach some level of competence on the basic technologies, it probably could not build very many. And the United States with regional allies might be able to preempt some before they could be launched. As such, the credible ability to shoot down just one, two, or three ballistic missiles in flight might well reduce the expected number of North Korean hits on American soil from one or two to perhaps zero. Neither side could truly know in advance what would happen in an actual war, of course. But Pyongyang might be less tempted to bother trying to develop such a missile capability if it thought the effort largely pointless due to expected American missile defense capabilities. And while North Korea might be able to develop countermeasures to fool many possible types of U.S. systems, such countermeasures can sometimes fail (or, possibly, be countered themselves by American technologies). So the United States should sustain and modernize its existing California/Alaska system.

Here is another example. China is dramatically improving its conventionally armed missile forces near western Pacific waters and thus near Taiwan. In a future crisis scenario, it could threaten airfields such as the Kadena Air Force Base on Okinawa, which would be crucial to any American role in helping defend Taiwan against Chinese attack. It is unrealistic to think that missile defense could make such an airfield impervious to missile strikes. But a combination of hardening of facilities, bolstering of runway-repair capabilities, deployment of versatile platforms that could operate in more austere conditions if necessary (such as vertical/ short-takeoff and landing, or VSTOL, aircraft), and missile defense might well sustain a credible and resilient American military capability well into the future. The odds of successful defense are even stronger in Guam, as it is further from the Chinese mainland, meaning that a system like the DF-21D "carrier killer" cannot reach it (though another missile, the DF-26, may be able to).[58]

This is not a case for trying to win an offense-defense arms race using American missile defense technologies. On balance, the offense will probably have the advantage in this kind of situation, at least until directed-energy defense systems or other types of new technological concepts for missile defense become effective and economical. Such systems are theoretically very appealing, since they do not suffer the same vulnerabilities to saturation attack as traditional missile-based defenses, and do not face the same cost-ratio disadvantages as a system that must use one or more defensive missiles to shoot down a given incoming missile. Although they remain in early stages of development, they could within one to two decades begin to provide considerable capabilities for site defense in particular. As such, research and development budgets for these technologies should remain robust. In the short term, though, a traditional missile defense system can make it harder for China or any other country to threaten a very limited use of force with confidence that it would achieve its desired coercive effects— because such a limited use of force might not penetrate even an imperfect and modestly sized defense.

Missile defense can also help protect ships in western Pacific waters—which China can now threaten with a variety of cruise and ballistic missiles including the SS-N-22 Sunburn, the SS-N-27 Sizzler, the DF-21D, and eventually the DF-26.[59] Chinese missile inventories are large relative to a given ship's defense capacities. But if China has trouble finding and targeting the ships, or if its missiles' guidance systems and targeting infrastructures can be jammed or otherwise compromised at least some of the time, missile defense may well be able to make a crucial contribution to fleet survival.

In addressing these and other possible threats and scenarios, today's U.S. Missile Defense Agency has a multifaceted plan with a combined price tag of about $9 billion annually (most spent through that agency, though some spent by the individual military services). There has been real restraint in the program; for example, earlier plans to build and deploy a number of airborne lasers aboard 747 aircraft have been shelved. But the guiding philosophy is still to address threats of different range, speed, and other flight characteristics with a variety of possible technologies that could vary depending on geographic milieu and other situational specifics. In other words, the United States seeks more than one system; it has concluded that it needs several, each in considerable quantities. They presently include the Patriot PAC-3 short-range air and missile defense system, the Terminal High Altitude Area Defense (THAAD) system, the Aegis/Standard Missile naval capabilities; and the long-range national missile defense system oriented around the ground-based interceptor and based in California and Alaska. The latter system is focused particularly on the potential North Korean threat though it could have utility against limited launches from other locations (even Iran) as well. Its near-term capability would include deploying 44 ground-based interceptors by 2017; improving the quality of those interceptors and their "kill vehicles" that home in on a target and collide with it to destroy it; and improving the radars used to guide the interceptors so as to better distinguish real warheads from fake decoys. [60]

Washington and Seoul may also be moving towards deployment of a THAAD battery on the Korean peninsula. Such a deployment makes sense in light of the North Korean threat. Given its limited range and capacity, it should not concern China. Nor should it be construed, or portrayed, by the United States and the Republic of Korea as a form of retaliation against Beijing for failing to sanction North Korea adequately in the aftermath of its nuclear and missile tests. American and Korean officials sometimes seem to send a message to China that deployment of THAAD would amount to such a quasi-punitive measure against Beijing; they should never do so because that inaccurately and unhelpfully confuses the purpose of the technology.

These missile defense systems are collectively showing considerable progress and displaying real capability. As of the fall of 2015, for example, according to a Lockheed Martin briefing, thirty-one of thirty-seven Aegis/Standard Missile tests had been successful, as well as fifty-three of sixty-one Patriot tests and eleven of eleven THAAD attempts.[61] All of these are based on so-called "hit-to-kill" technology in which an interceptor is steered directly into the path of an incoming missile or warhead; the resulting impact, typically at several kilometers per second relative speed, suffices to destroy the threat. As far as these technologies have come, however, there remain two main structural limitations with them, and even the planned upgrades to current systems will not be able to alter the situation fundamentally. First, they are vulnerable to decoys that can mimic warheads, especially in the vacuum of outer space where air resistance does not affect flight trajectories. Second, they are expensive. Each defensive shot requires an interceptor typically costing millions of dollars, which is tolerable against a small threat, but is not cost-effective against an opponent with a large offensive missile inventory. Thus, the limitations of missile defense systems must be kept just as vividly in planners' minds as their attributes, and ambitions for large-scale deployments vetted carefully against cost.

CHAPTER 5

The Wars

Not all changes to U.S. defense policy should involve cutbacks. Indeed, the United States needs to do modestly more in the conflicts of the broader Middle East. President Obama has been moving in this general direction himself, with a 50 percent funding increase proposed for the 2017 war budget for the fight against ISIL and a recent decision to prolong the U.S. military presence in Afghanistan. But these worthy steps are not yet enough.

Naturally, the United States will have to stay flexible in how it handles crises and conflicts abroad, since by definition they are contingencies that cannot be fully foreseen or mapped out in advance. Nonetheless, I am confident in asserting that the next U.S. president will need to do more about two particular elements of the broader Middle East and the so-called war on terror. Both will involve using somewhat more American military power—though with the necessary increases in troops measured in the thousands, not the many tens or hundreds of thousands. The two places in question are Afghanistan and Syria—two of the areas that former Chairman of the Joint Chiefs of Staff Martin Dempsey emphasized in proposing his concept of a network of regional bases that could serve as strongholds and operational facilities in an ongoing struggle against extremism. This concept has gained some currency in the course of 2015 and 2016 with the Obama Administration. But there are still gaps in needed capabilities.

Although I do not treat them in detail here, there are other plausible uses of increased U.S. power abroad in the years to come as well. Iraq is the most obvious example; at present, the development of the Iraqi army is going tolerably well but still fairly slowly. [1] There is a case for more American trainers—perhaps even to help build an Iraqi National Guard, should the Iraqi parliament finally decide to authorize its creation—and also for more American advisers at the brigade level and in the role of tactical air controllers within the regular Army as it seeks to liberate areas that ISIL currently controls.

There are other cases in point as well. At some point, an overdue international effort to help train a Libyan army will be needed—and direct action against a growing ISIL presence there may be required even sooner. There is also a case for deploying mentoring teams to work with the Nigerian military, now undergoing significant and promising reforms under a new president, Muhammadu Buhari, in its struggle against Boko Haram, a declared affiliate of ISIL itself. (Further afield, though less relevant to the struggle against Takfiri/Salafist extremism, there could be a case for deploying an "advise and assist" brigade of American troops to support the UN peacekeeping mission in the Democratic Republic of Congo, if a new president to succeed Joseph Kabila is elected and shows promise.)[2]

Taken together, the resulting increases in American military power abroad are likely to keep annual overseas contingency operations or OCO budgets in the range of $50 billion to $60 billion as they have been in recent years. I do not believe that needed troops, or costs, should grow substantially beyond that unless there is ultimately a peace deal and resulting international peace implementation force for Syria. At that point, there could be a case for a temporary need for 10,000 to 25,000 U.S. troops as part of an international force, though those figures should decline within one to two years.

AFGHANISTAN

Before getting to policy recommendations, it is useful to review the overall situation in Afghanistan today.

To be sure, the security situation in Afghanistan is bad. Yet it is hardly catastrophic. The UN estimates that war is causing about 10,000 casualties a year at present, of which perhaps 3,000 are deaths—higher than at any time records have been kept this century. Statistically at least, however, that is still a lower death rate from violence than countries supposedly at peace, like South Africa, or countries that have come to be seen as success stories, like Colombia. Afghan cities still bustle; markets and schools are still open; the population is not cowering in fear in most of the country.[3]

Afghan security forces let Kunduz fall to the enemy in the autumn of 2015, but then they retook it within a couple weeks. Subsequently, they stopped the December Taliban attack on the Kandahar airfield, even if not before thirty-five civilians lost their lives. They also repulsed coordinated Taliban probes against a number of other regional centers in the immediate aftermath of the Kunduz disaster. Earlier in that same year, moreover, the Afghan army planned and conducted three major operations essentially on its own, two of them involving multiple corps (each corps is about 25,000 strong, with specific geographic responsibilities). The Taliban remain resilient, and gained some net holdings in 2015 and then into early 2016—but probably not more than 3 to 5 percent of the country as measured by affected population.

The Afghan people are worried but not desperate. In a recent Asia Foundation survey, they expressed more concern about the country's future than at any other time in the last decade. Indeed, only 37 percent expressed optimism, down starkly from 54 percent in 2014, when elections and the presidential transition process were taking place. However, a substantial majority—75 percent, essentially unchanged from the recent past—expressed contentment and happiness with their lives despite it all. That is partly a reflection of the positive attributes of the Afghan people. It also may reflect their view that, as bad as things are, the nation is not on the verge of collapse. While two-thirds say the security situation is not good, more than two-thirds express confidence in their nation's army and police.[4]

On the question of numbers for 2017 and beyond, the United States and NATO in general will retain assets for intelligence, commando raids against certain types of targets, central training of Afghan forces, and limited air operations. U.S. forces will be based at five major operating locations in the east and south of the country, plus a half dozen sites in and around Kabul; European militaries will concentrate in the nation's north and west. But in order to comply with President Obama's ceiling of 5,500 American troops come 2017, NATO will have to pull advisors out of the forward headquarters of the Army's main field-level assets—the 201st, 203rd, 205th, 207th, 209th, and 215th corps. In fact, as recent challenges from Kunduz to Helmand to the nation's east attest, unexpected crises can erupt with little warning. The corps in Helmand province and the kandak (or battalion) near Kunduz that experienced some of the greatest setbacks in 2015 were not benefiting from advising, mentoring, and partnering at the time of their most severe problems. That defect has been temporarily remedied, and NATO is working to help Afghans rebuild the 215th corps in Helmand, but by 2017 it will no longer have adequate forces to carry out such efforts.

For all his commendable resolve, Obama is still making mistakes in his Afghan policy. He is still trying so hard to minimize the U.S. role and wean Afghans from international help that he runs unnecessary risks of losing the war in the short term. None of Obama's thinking is reckless. But it pushes too far and too fast for an Afghan people and government who are still making several huge transitions, in political and economic as well as security terms, that leave their situation very fraught and fragile. In particular, the United States and NATO-led coalition should make two changes to existing security plans as promptly as possible— and if President Obama does not spearhead them, his successor should.

First, U.S. and NATO airpower should be allowed to target the Taliban, as I have argued recently with retired General David Petraeus, former header of the International Security Assistance Force.[5] In recent years, and especially since the NATO-led mission in Afghanistan changed from the International Security Assistance Force to Resolute Support in December of 2014, Washington has restricted its use of combat power to two purposes: targeting al Qaeda (and now also ISIL, as of early 2016), and providing self-defense for NATO troops. Sometimes in a pinch, the United States has helped Afghan forces when they were in desperate straits, as with the battle over Kunduz in the fall of 2015. But generally speaking, rules of engagement have been very narrowly construed in an effort to encourage the Afghan armed forces to defend their own territory.

That goal is a seemingly reasonable proposition. However, taking this approach now places unrealistically high demands on Afghan forces at this juncture in their development. They have already had to adjust to a 90 percent reduction in the strength of NATO troops over the last three years, even as the Taliban threat has remained resilient. Their air force remains at roughly half to two-thirds strength, in terms of pilots and airframes, according to the 1225 Report issued by the Pentagon in late 2015. That lag is due to a conscious decision made by NATO several years ago, since NATO understandably desired to build the Afghan army and police up first and the Afghan air force subsequently. Progress is being made towards redressing existing gaps; in fact, Afghan air forces increased their pace of aerial attacks by more than 1,000 percent in 2015, relative to the year before. But it will take the rest of the decade to complete the job. Given these realities, Taliban forces have learned that they can mass in the field with relative impunity from overhead attack in many cases.

Also, there are unholy alliances, shifting memberships, and various pledges of allegiance linking key extremist groups in South Asia—al Qaeda, ISIL, and the Taliban, as well as Lashkar-e-Taiba, the Islamic Movement of Uzbekistan, and the Pakistani Taliban (or TTP). Making too fine a distinction of which extremist groups the United States, and NATO, can attack within Afghanistan and which they cannot fails to recognize that at least the above six are fairly united in common ideology and often in common purpose.

The second major change that is needed in U.S. security policy in Afghanistan concerns the size and capabilities of American forces there. The planned reduction to 5,500 U.S. troops by January 1, 2017, will almost certainly be premature. Indeed, the United States should actually expand its forces, as soon as possible, to 12,000 to 15,000 for a couple years. (Either way, American troops will be joined by up to several thousand more NATO forces from at least two dozen countries. The alliance in general is showing remarkable patience with this prolonged mission. That said, there are also inherent limits on how far non-U.S. partners will go in building up their capacities; any buildup will have to be U.S.-led, alas.) That would allow NATO to advise and mentor, in the field, all key Afghan army corps and even some select brigades and kandaks that are under particular duress or experiencing particular problems.

More generally, Washington and Brussels should stop making an exit strategy their top priority in Afghanistan security policy. They should emphasize instead the importance of an enduring partnership between NATO and Afghanistan. The alliance's counterterrorism goals support such an approach. And by taking a longer-term view for planning, the United States and foreign partners can steady some nerves in Afghanistan itself while also sending a message to the Taliban and Pakistan that NATO's resolve and patience are firm. This message can shape the incentives of various actors and thereby help the prospects of the broader mission. The next U.S. president should create a four-year plan for continuing the mission in Afghanistan; during that time, troop levels should not decline appreciably. He or she should also underscore that even after the four years, NATO forces would remain in the country, though perhaps at somewhat lower numbers by that point.

Fortunately, President Obama's timetable for downsizing forces will allow most of ongoing mentoring relationships with Afghan army corps to continue through 2016 and another fighting season. Given the Taliban threat, that is crucially important militarily. It is also important politically. It could help buy time for President Ghani and Chief Executive Abdullah as well as other Afghan political leaders to get through what will likely be another tough transition year on the political front. Already, parliamentary elections are overdue. In addition, the temporary powersharing arrangement that Ghani and Abdullah fashioned with Secretary Kerry's help in 2014 is due to expire in the fall of 2016. The simplest path forward may be to encourage the simple extension of that time horizon, and perhaps even a further delay in parliamentary elections if the delay can be utilized to strengthen the country's independent election commission and voting procedures (and perhaps change the so-called single nontransferable voting system). But even if further delays are acceptable, they will have to be the result of a conscious decision of key actors. A steady and stabilizing security arrangement will likely be helpful in facilitating such a crucial political decision.

SYRIA

U.S. policy towards Syria since the Arab spring uprisings of 2011 has failed comprehensively. President Assad has not been driven from power, and Russia's recent intervention has strengthened his hand; ISIL has emerged as the strongest part of the anti-Assad resistance; at least 300,000 people have died and half the country's pre-war population of 23 million has been driven from their homes, with hundreds of thousands now reaching western Europe; peace talks have predictably failed to produce a lasting accord.

The ascendance of the Islamic State in Iraq and the Levant (ISIL) as the major element of the opposition to the Bashar al-Assad regime may not yet amount to an imminent existential threat to American security. Indeed, very few Americans have died to date at the hands of ISIL or affiliates. But ISIL's rise does place at much greater risk the security of Iraq, the future of Syria itself, and the stability of Lebanon and Jordan.[6] The ideology of ISIL, as with al Qaeda, is extremist, ruthless, and ultimately very expansive in its geographic ambition. These groups jeopardize the safety of individual American citizens right now, even if not western nations as a whole. The Charlie Hebdo, Paris, San Bernardino, and Brussels tragedies have all had links or inspiration from ISIL and/or al Qaeda. Sanctuaries in Syria and Iraq provide ISIL (and also the al-Nusra Front, the al Qaeda operation in Syria) areas where it can organize, plot, train, and financially and logistically support those who can subsequently carry out-large scale attacks in the West.[7] Some 56 Americans were charged in ISIL-related activities in 2015, a record number that demonstrates the danger to the U.S. homeland.[8] ISIL recruiting efforts may continue to bring about 1,000 new fighters a month from all over the world to the Syria/Iraq/Mideast battlefield.[9] This pace appears to be roughly adequate to replenish the loss rate from U.S.-led airstrikes.[10] By early 2016, the Director of National Intelligence estimated that over the course of the war, at least 38,200 foreign fighters, including at least 6,900 from the West, had traveled to Syria, coming from a grand total of 120 countries. Moreover, ISIL is now aided by communications mechanisms that are increasingly impervious to outside intelligence gathering efforts.[11] Put all this together, and it is entirely credible, even if unlikely, that hundreds or even thousands of Americans could die at the hands of ISIL in coming years. It is also imaginable that even worse could happen, such as a successful ISIL attack on a nuclear power plant or toxic chemical weapons facility.

What U.S. policy would make more sense? Counterintuitively, the only credible path forward may be a plan that in effect deconstructs Syria. But doing this will require more military capability, including up to several thousand Americans on the ground within certain parts of Syria. Specifically, the international community should work to create pockets of more viable security and governance within Syria over time. With initial footholds in place, the strategy could develop further into a type of "ink-spot" campaign that eventually seeks to join the various local initiatives into a broader and more integrated effort.

This approach builds on current U.S. strategy, but with a much less glaring mismatch between means and ends. Requiring ideological purity of opposition fighters before the United States trains them would no longer be done as stringently. Requiring that they were untainted by any past associations with extremists would no longer be a central element of the vetting process either. Ideally, the U.S. Congress would explicitly endorse these changed criteria, in order to accept ownership of a policy that would have its own risks.

The idea would be to help moderate elements establish and eventually declare, reliable "safe zones" within Syria once they were able. American, as well as Saudi, Turkish, British, Jordanian, and other Arab forces would act in support, not only from the air, but increasingly on the ground via the presence of special forces as well. The approach would benefit from Syria's open desert terrain, which could allow creation of buffer zones that would be monitored through a combination of technologies, patrols, and other methods that outside special forces could help Syrian local fighters set up.

Were Assad foolish enough to challenge these zones, even if he somehow forced the withdrawal of the outside special forces, he would be likely to lose his airpower in ensuing retaliatory strikes by outside forces, depriving his military of one of its few advantages over ISIL. Thus, he would be unlikely to do this.

Creation of these sanctuaries would produce autonomous zones that would never again have to face the prospect of rule by either Assad or ISIL. They would also constitute areas where humanitarian relief could be supplied, schools reopened, and larger opposition fighting forces recruited, trained, and based. UN agencies and NGOs would help in the effort to the extent possible, focusing on health, education, and basic economic recovery in the first instance. Governing councils would be formed, more likely by appointment than election, to help international agencies make decisions on key matters relevant to rudimentary governance. Regardless of details, relief could certainly be provided far more effectively than is the case today. At least one such area should be contiguous to Jordan and one to Turkey, and be created in cooperation with Amman and Ankara. These locations would allow secure transportation lines for humanitarian as well as military supplies. They would also provide bases from which to attack ISIL in its strongholds, a mission that Western forces could carry out in conjunction with local allies.

The ultimate end-game for these zones would not have to be determined in advance. But it would be highly advantageous, and help deconflict America's interaction with other key outside players including Russia, Turkey, Jordan, and the Gulf states, to establish the general goal of a confederal Syria consisting of several highly autonomous zones rather than a strong and centralized federal government as in the past. One of those zones might be primarily for Alawites and perhaps many Christians as well. But all would have to ensure minority rights including property rights. None could be for ISIL or al-Nusra. Assad and his inner circle could go into exile or relocate into the Alawite sector. "Accidental guerrillas," to use David Kilcullen's memorable phrase, who had previously been in cahoots with extremist groups could in some cases be forgiven their transgressions, if there were reason to think that they were dependable. Some of the initial safe zones, after growing and expanding, could eventually merge. A future national government, if it could be pieced together through negotiation, would ideally be formed someday. But it would have only a modest role in such a confederal arrangement.

At some point, the confederation would likely require support from an international peacekeeping force. The United States should be willing to commit to being part of a force, since without it, it is dubious that the conflict's various parties will have confidence in the stability of any settlement. Moreover, that force would likely have to be large; Syria is several times the size of Bosnia, where the initial NATO deployment exceeded 50,000 troops (though it was probably oversized for the mission). In the case of Syria a total international force of 100,000, deployed primarily along lines of separation between autonomous zones and in the intermixed central cities, might be required. Alternatively, a more modest mission of say 20,000 to 50,000 troops could be deployed, but there would be greater risks associated with that more modest footprint.

The estimated short-term troop requirement of several thousand Americans, along with commensurate numbers of trainers and special forces from countries such as Jordan, Turkey, Britain, and the Gulf states, is based on the concepts of training, mentoring, and carrying out limited direct action, all the while maintaining reasonable perimeter security and self-defense capability for any locations that are established. Specifically, as is also seen in the current plan for Afghanistan, individual concentrations of foreign advisors and forces would typically involve 500 or somewhat more personnel per site. Establishing such sites in the Kurdish north, Druse southwest, Southern-Front dominated regions, and at least one or two areas in the north and central zones where Sunni forces predominate would lead in broad terms to this potential size for American forces, on top of capabilities already in the region. Initially, force sizes would be smaller, measured in the hundreds, since they would have to be careful about where they established footholds and be most attentive to force protection considerations. But even these smaller contingents would help with humanitarian relief, signal that the United States was seriously committed to changing battlefield dynamics—and also therefore improve the prospects for negotiations, perhaps even sooner than might be initially expected. A peacekeeping force, if ultimately deployed, might require perhaps 10,000 to 25,000 Americans for a modest period.

CHAPTER 6

Reforms and Efficiencies

Beyond specific changes to weapons and forces, there is also the broader issue of how the Department of Defense, still a sprawling if somewhat downsized behemoth, can make itself more efficient. Such efforts must remain front and center for the next president and his or her team.

MILITARY COMPENSATION

The United States is a democracy at war asking young men and women to volunteer to defend the country and its security. Few would deny that the United States has a special debt to its troops who answer that call, and that it should take good care of them.

The country also has the best military in history—and that is not an American birthright, as we know from other periods in history, like the immediate post-Vietnam days of the so-called "hollow force." Rather, it is largely because of the very high quality of men and women in uniform at present. The country must continue to make military service appealing enough that such individuals continue to join, and remain in, the force.

The American military is good largely because it is an adaptive, learning organization. It has a tradition, going back to Vietnam, of training realistically and then carrying out "after action reviews" in which everyone is expected to be self-critical. It does this in wartime extremely well too. But this is only possible because resources are adequate to train realistically and because the military's educational and compensation systems are good enough to attract many of our best and brightest into national service.[1]

Fortunately, there is no systematic military-civilian pay gap that works against U.S. military personnel today. Private-sector wages, especially for middle-class and blue-collar jobs, have stagnated in recent decades in the United States while military compensation has continued to improve. Moreover, military jobs carry additional benefits above and beyond wages that further favor those in uniform. On average, for individuals of a given age and educational background, the American armed forces actually pay substantially *better* today than does the private sector. Averaged across the military, and counting all benefits except pensions, enlisted military personnel make more than 90 percent of their comparable cohorts in the civilian population—that is, those with similar age, experience, and educational qualifications. This situation is generally similar for officers.[2] Military compensation per active-duty service member, according to a 2012 Congressional Budget Office study, increased to roughly $100,000 in 2012 from $70,000 in 2000.[3] (These costs do not include the dramatically higher expenditures for Veterans' Administration benefits that one would expect, and that the country should fully support for those individuals and for the families of individuals who have been hurt or killed in war.)

There is no case, however, for substantial cuts in military compensation. Beyond the desirability of attracting very good people to the armed forces, other factors argue for keeping compensation solid. For example, military spouses often have trouble finding work, given the frequent changes of assignment of their husbands and wives, meaning that family income may not do as well comparatively as the average income of a member of the military.[4]

Thus, I favor keeping basic military compensation steady in real-dollar terms. General increases in real pay are not needed in the foreseeable future. But pay should go up with the rate of inflation, and bonuses of various types used to address specific shortfalls in the force structure.

An option that would generate savings would eliminate stateside military exchanges and commissaries (an idea the Obama administration does not endorse in its 2017 budget). These kinds of on-base stores are popular with military families, but in the era of Walmart, Costco, Home Depot, and Best Buy, they are less important than before and a less prudent use of taxpayers' money. At least $1.5 billion a year can be saved in this way.[5] As a compromise, some exchanges and commissaries could be retained in those few locations where large commercial outlets are absent.

Even bigger savings can be found by increasing cost sharing within the military health care program. The TRI-CARE system provides an extremely good deal to military families. While this has been understandable to a degree, it has arguably gone too far, not only far exceeding the generosity of plans in the civilian economy, but incentivizing excessive use of health care (due to the low costs).

One of the issues is that TRICARE is available to retirees and their families. Some retirees insist that this benefit remain as is, arguing that they were promised free health care for life when joining the military. Well, if they were, it was in many cases a type of health care radically different—and radically cheaper, perhaps by 75 percent or more depending on their age—than what is available today. No one would begrudge wounded warriors the best of care; the issue here, rather, is the cost-sharing system of copayments and enrollment fees for the typical military family or military retiree family. Reforms that retained a generous military health care system but with somewhat greater cost-sharing, especially by retirees, could save perhaps $2 billion to as much as $5 billion a year relative to 2017 administration plans and the current system. The savings might be phased in, however, saving less in early years. Military health care would still be a very good bargain compared with private-sector plans with such an approach, as it should be.[6]

And finally, it is simply time to change the military retirement system, going back to ideas temporarily implemented under Ronald Reagan in the 1980s. The military retirement system is arguably too generous at twenty years of service and not generous enough for those leaving the armed forces sooner. Indeed, those leaving the military after one, two, or three tours of duty get nothing—an unfairness to many of our combat veterans, among others. The generous benefits for those staying within DoD for twenty years continue despite the fact that second careers after the military have become much more common, and military pay relative to private sector pay is much better than before. This situation may be particularly ripe for change for officers, whose military salaries and benefits are higher than for others, and whose post-military careers are often better-paying as well. Providing a modest benefit, analogous to a 401K in the private sector, or eligibility for military personnel to participate in the Thrift Savings Plan available to civilian government employees (which involves matching government funds for those willing to save for retirement), would improve fairness. (Higher amounts could be contributed by the government for those who have served in dangerous zones.) Such a concept was legislated in the 2016 National Defense Authorization Act but only in a very modest way; real financial support for the 401k/TSP option by the government would make it much more meaningful.

This new retirement system could be designed to save money. The Perry/Hadley independent panel that assessed the Pentagon's 2010 Quadrennial Defense Review made this general argument. A recent Defense Business Board study suggests savings that could approach $10 billion a year over the next twenty years. However, in light of political realities, I would propose a more modest reform—a cost-neutral change that would have the government contribute to the 401k-like accounts of all military personnel and reduce the standard twenty-year pension (particularly for better-paid personnel) by whatever relatively modest amount were needed to afford the 401K plans, building on the concept enacted in the 2016 Defense Act. Thus, I propose this policy not as a way of saving money in the Department of Defense, but as a way of promoting fairness and making service more appealing to those who do not intend to make it a career. The Obama administration has made a somewhat similar proposal in its 2017 budget.[7]

EFFICIENCIES AND REFORMS

There are also ways to save money in Pentagon business practices—how the Department of Defense manages its vast network of organizations and facilities across the country and indeed the world.

Consider three key ideas. First is something called performance-based logistics. Second is "strategic sourcing," and third is the hardy perennial of base closures.

The basic logic of performance-based logistics is fairly simple, and rather elegant from the point of view of theoretical economics. It is already employed in 5 to 10 percent of all Pentagon maintenance contracts as well. Traditionally, the Department of Defense has paid contractors to repair equipment on a transactional basis—that is, fee for service. When something would break, it would then be fixed. Contractors would make more money the more repairs they conducted. This system gives contractors no direct financial incentive to make repairs more efficiently, and it also often reduces the availability of key equipment since much of it is frequently in the shop.[8]

By contrast, a performance-based logistics (PBL) contract pays a contractor per successful flight-hour, steaming day, or mile driven of a plane, ship, or vehicle. It leaves it to the contractor to figure out the optimal schedule for doing repairs as well as preventive maintenance. It thereby encourages the contractor to bundle maintenance activities into a single visit to the shop so that many things can be done efficiently and economically at once. This system also leads contractors to do more detailed studies on which parts tend to break most often so that they can perhaps be reengineered or otherwise made more durable.

Savings from this approach typically range in the vicinity of 5 to 20 percent. There can also be second-order savings from other effects of successful PBLs. For example, if aircraft are available a higher percentage of the time, the DoD will not need to buy as many to ensure that a given number are ready to go on any given day. As such, not only maintenance costs (funded in the DoD's Operations and Maintenance or O&M budget) but also equipment purchase costs (funded in Procurement) can be reduced.

There are some cases where PBL may not be applicable. This could be the case for brand new systems using innovative technology (since no dependable baseline exists for knowing likely maintenance costs in such cases, making a PBL a gamble for all parties), or for systems about to be retired (since it takes time to set up a PBL and make it efficient). But on balance, over time, up to $70 billion or $80 billion of annual O&M costs could perhaps be addressed through the PBL approach, meaning that later in the 2020s, a systematic use of this approach might yield the DoD annual recurring savings in excess of $5 billion. Shorter-term savings will be more modest, given the need to apply this concept carefully and individually to each major system—so I would estimate savings of only $1 billion annually by 2020.

Strategic sourcing is the idea of buying in bulk, across as much of the government or at least the DoD as possible. How much could be saved in this way? The Government Accountability Office recently estimated that possible savings could reach up to $5 billion eventually.[9] As a practical matter, strategic sourcing has to happen case by case, it works much better for certain types of supplies than others, and it needs to be done well if savings are to result—so in the short term, savings would be modest. But the effort needs to be undertaken more diligently than now appears to be the case. Again, $1 billion in annual savings seems a safer target for 2020.

Finally, consider base closures. The Obama administration still encourages, in its 2017 budget request, another Base Realignment and Closure (BRAC) round in 2019, and it is right to do so. The first four rounds, in 1988, 1991, 1993, and 1995, were collectively a success. They were admittedly more expensive to implement than initially foreseen (with a combined up-front cost of $25 billion), and slower to yield savings, but still a net benefit to the DoD and the taxpayer over time. However, the 2005 round, originally expected to yield $35 billion in savings over twenty years, is now expected to net just $10 billion, with most of those savings towards the end of the process. Initial implementation costs, originally projected at $21 billion, wound up closer to $35 billion.[10] Some of these unfavorable revisions to original estimates may have been due to the fact that a fifth round of base closures had fewer obvious targets for major savings than the first four; some of it frankly could have been due to questionable analysis, planning, and implementation by the BRAC Commission, and perhaps too much emphasis on promoting "jointness" across the services in this round rather than on simple efficiency.

The DoD still has 20 percent more infrastructure than its current force posture requires. It has dramatically reduced infrastructure in Europe since the Cold War; it has also closed or realigned about 130 major facilities in the United States in the five BRAC rounds noted above. Its remaining real estate includes 241 installations categorized as "large or medium," with 205 in the United States and territories as well as another thirty-six abroad. Or, to use a different categorization, the DoD says it has 513 "major installations" worldwide— and a grand total of 4,855 sites of all sizes and types globally (4,268 of those in the United States and territories).[11] More base closures are needed—at least one if not two more rounds. Future rounds could be expected to do better than the 2005 round, if they are allowed to return to their earlier mandate of emphasizing efficiency (though local economic conditions might be given somewhat greater emphasis in making decisions on which bases to close in future rounds as well, since some communities have an easier time adjusting to closures than others). A future round will likely yield eventual savings of $2 billion to $3 billion a year, like each of the first four rounds.[12] That said, net savings over a decade would be very modest as those types of savings tend not to be realized quickly. So, base closures are a worthy idea, but a gift to posterity more than a means of addressing near-term Pentagon funding shortfalls.[13]

ACQUISITION REFORM FOR A SYSTEM ¾ GOOD, ¼ BROKEN

The topic of acquisition reform has been a major focus of the Obama Pentagon, especially with Under Secretary of Defense for Acquisition, Logistics, and Technology Frank Kendall and his "better buying power" initiatives. It was also a major focus of Congress in 2015, with Chairmen Mac Thornberry and John McCain leading their respective armed services committees in the House and Senate to pass a defense authorization bill that encouraged some reforms, including returning a greater share of responsibility for acquisitions to the military services rather than the Office of the Secretary of Defense. Where do things stand, and how much money might be saved?

On balance, I think that modest savings are eventually possible through acquisition reform. But in the spirit of the Congressional Budget Office, I would not "score" any savings officially—it is too soon to expect major savings from ongoing changes and too hard to quantify any that might result, except for modest reductions in the acquisition workforce as discussed below. Nor should savings be the main goal. Getting needed technology into the warfighter's hands promptly is at least as important—and the Department of Defense needs to institutionalize some of the methods, decision-making groups, and budgetary devices that it has employed so far this century for that purpose for similar situations in the future.[14]

Here is the context. The American defense debate is afflicted by a certain fundamental contradiction about how the Pentagon buys its weapons and other equipment, and about the state of America's defense industrial base.

On the one hand, the media narrative often fixates on horror stories concerning $600 toilet seats, billion-dollar aircraft and ships, fighter jets costing three times what was originally expected, and programs canceled for poor performance.

But there is a happier side of the story to tell as well. Whenever they go into combat, American armed forces have the best equipment in the world. This has been true since World War II, and it constitutes a huge strategic advantage for the United States—as seen, most notably, in Operation Desert Storm in 1991, the opening stages of the Afghanistan and Iraq wars in 2001 and 2003 respectively, and the quieter successes of deterrence policy in places like the east Asian littoral in recent decades. Whether overhyped or not, all the talk of a revolution in military affairs in the last quarter century has largely been the result of breakthroughs in stealth, satellites, precision-guided munitions, drones, computing, and other high-technology capabilities that have given the American soldier, sailor, airman, airwoman, and Marine enormous advantages against their enemies. Moreover, in modern times, the United States has bought all these capabilities while spending 3 to 5 percent of gross domestic product on its military, roughly half the average (or less) than in Eisenhower's day. U.S. weapons manufacturers also lead the world in arms exports, suggesting that it is not just Americans who see the value in what the U.S. defense industrial base develops and produces.

As the defense budget has declined, so has the size and shape of the industrial base. What was a huge national resource in World War II, when most major American industries were legally required to contribute to the war effort, became a more streamlined version of the same system in the Cold-War years. Since the Cold War ended, however, many companies have gotten out of the defense business, leaving most weapons production to a handful of prime contractors focused mostly on the military mission. The broad flow of ideas, technologies, and personnel back and forth between civilian and defense worlds that characterized the middle decades of the twentieth century is now largely gone.[15] Residual defense industry remains very impressive, and a national treasure. But in areas such as fighter jet, bomber, space launch, submarine, and aircraft carrier technology, the United States is generally down to just two or sometimes just one main producer. And in new realms such as cyber, where generational changes in technology occur every couple of years rather than every couple of decades or longer, the reams of federal acquisition regulations and the slow pace of the defense acquisition and contracting world leave America's armed forces at risk of falling seriously behind the times.

What to do? How to fix the system without throwing the baby out with the bathwater? How to retain all that is working well in defense acquisition—preserving the cutting-edge character and high quality of most American weapons—while building a viable system for the twenty-first century that is innovative and affordable?

My main argument is that the acquisition system of the DoD is in fact fairly good. In fact, overall, it is excellent, if by the system one means the overall performance of the country's laboratories, main defense contractors, and military personnel who then operate the equipment that the U.S. taxpayer has purchased for them.

But if it is excellent, it is three-fourths so. There are major remaining problems. Some involve a tendency still to over-insure by buying weaponry that is more expensive than need be at times. This problem arises at the high strategic levels of the decision making of the military service chiefs and their civilian leadership; it is less a weakness of the acquisition system itself. Other problems arise from the excessive bureaucracy and red tape associated with the acquisition process, which drive away certain types of potential providers whose technologies could be of great benefit to the U.S. armed forces.

The situation was captured pithily in a session at Brookings on April 13, 2015. Under Secretary Kendall rated the U.S. military acquisition system as meriting a high grade—a B+, maybe even an A-. Former Deputy Secretary Bill Lynn, now CEO of DRS/Finnmeccanica USA, agreed with that grade if one was referring to major weapons platforms. But he gave the system a C- or so for anything involving computers, information technology, and Moore's Law. He also argued for taking better advantage of opportunities for more economical purchases of equipment that might be provided by foreign firms, smaller firms, and nontraditional providers in some cases. These were of course simplified and notional depictions. But they do capture the essence of the strengths and weaknesses of the existing system in a memorable way. And in so doing, they help point the way forward towards next steps in reform:

- Use Federal Acquisition Regulations (FAR) Title 12 more often, rather than falling back on Federal Acquisition Regulations Title 15. In theory, the Pentagon is supposed to buy commercial goods, as under the so-called FAR 12 code, whenever possible, and avoid the complex and cumbersome FAR 15 rules that involve negotiated contracts. In these FAR 12 cases, the Pentagon can, in theory, behave like a normal customer and avoid the complex steps and onerous paperwork involved in a major weapons procurement process. But the tendency is still to define requirements in such a way that there are enough military-unique characteristics for whatever radio, phone, jeep, or computer is at issue that the FAR 15 code is used almost by default.

■ Streamline oversight when the Pentagon can rely on competition to discipline firms about price. Today, for example, the Defense Contracts Management Agency has an on-site presence in many factories; its personnel tabulate what it thinks weapons should cost, based on all sorts of details about the production process. This may make sense for complex weapons being built by just one supplier. But for cases in which there is a commercial equivalent or two producers, the competitive process can provide the discipline—just as it does in the commercial market— and oversight can be scaled back enormously. The DoD can base its future-years purchases of a given weapon in part on which of two companies may be providing a better buy at present. This change could in fact gradually save a modest amount of money, since it could allow for a reduction in the size of the 150,000-strong DoD acquisition workforce, though I would not forecast savings soon enough to be relevant over a five-year time horizon.

■ Follow the JIEDDO model for other technologies. When so many Americans were being hurt or killed by improvised explosive devices in Iraq and Afghanistan, Congress allowed the DoD to create special, expedited acquisition procedures and ultimately the Joint Improvised-Explosive-Device Defeat Organization to research and produce relevant technologies quickly. Deputy Secretary of Defense Paul Wolfowitz and others championed the effort, to great effect. This concept could be used, especially for lower-risk technologies that nonetheless are important to build quickly. Another way of getting at the same concept is through existing procedures known as "Other Transaction Authority." These approaches could save money in areas such as information technology, on the one hand, where the pace of change is fast—or, on the other hand, areas such as ground vehicles, where technologies are largely mature.

- Break down information technology purchases into smaller batches. There are times when creating a huge common computer infrastructure with the same machines or software across hundreds of thousands of users may make sense. There are other cases where this big approach puts too many eggs in one basket. By using open-architecture and modularity concepts, making sure different systems can talk to each other but allowing more discrete and smaller buys by various agencies, the DoD may do better. Over time, this too could save money—particularly by avoiding future white-elephant projects that wind up costing the taxpayer enormously yet do not work that well.

- For commercial technologies or close derivatives of commercial systems, allow firms to keep their intellectual property rights rather than sharing all relevant data with the government. In such cases, the government cannot really claim to have generated the relevant expertise and information, so it makes more sense to keep it proprietary. This principle could apply from aircraft engines to smart phones to space boosters. It could help convince many companies wary of doing business with the Pentagon to reassess. However, it should not be employed in cases where a specialized defense system is developed by a given company at considerable taxpayer expense, especially in cases where the DoD may wish to contract for upgrades or modifications subsequently—because in such cases, competition could be thwarted by such retention of intellectual property rights.

Defense acquisition reform has been a major preoccupation of planners for more than half a century—and will likely remain that way for at least as long into the future—given the complex nature of the defense research, development, and procurement enterprise. But even gradual, incremental progress is worth striving for—and it is also of considerable value to the taxpayer, the armed forces, and the nation. And in some areas such as IT acquisition, where the technologies are newer and the rate of change faster, the opportunities may be particularly ripe for exploitation if the DoD can truly learn to do business better. The system is not broken. But to truly deserve a grade of B+ or A-, it can and must still do much better.

THE DOD'S UNIFIED COMMAND PLAN

A final topic of interest, though with only the most minor of budgetary significance, concerns how the U.S. Armed Forces organize for various types of operations, particularly those abroad. Senator John McCain, Chairman of the Senate Armed Services Committee, held a number of hearings on the subject in late 2015, and the issue seems likely to remain on the policy-making radar screen. Recently, the new Chairman of the Joint Chiefs of Staff, General Joseph Dunford, expressed interest in reform himself.

Some changes are likely in order, perhaps most of all in the cyber domain. While the DoD appears to be improving its cybersecurity considerably,[16] even a modest chance of an entire warfighting network being incapacitated in a crisis is very concerning. Moreover, transportation and logistics systems that depend on civilian infrastructure to support combat troops are likely even more vulnerable. General Dunford's idea to streamline his own joint staff, housed in the Pentagon, also makes sense. That is more a question of tight management than fundamental reorganization, however.

On balance, I am a skeptic about major changes in the Unified Command Plan and most other large-scale transformations that could come from a "Goldwater Nichols II," some thirty years after the initial effort. In an era when the government has been seemingly reorganizing itself to deal with every new problem, most notably with intelligence and homeland security, we need to avoid change for change's sake.

Under the Unified Command Plan, the Pentagon divides up overseas responsibilities into six geographic sectors (there are also three functional commands, each with global responsibilities in specific aspects of warfare—special operations, transportation, and strategic/space matters). Africa Command and European Command each have responsibility for more than fifty countries. Pacific Command covers half the globe by area and, with China, India, and Indonesia, nearly that large a fraction by population (with some thirty-six nations). Central Command has seen much of the combat action this century (though it has "only" twenty countries within its area of responsibility). Southern Command works with the thirty-one countries of Latin America south of Mexico. Northern Command deals with our own hemisphere, largely in regard to homeland security matters.

Each command is run by a four-star general or admiral who has likely worked on other parts of the world as well during his career (at present, there is not a woman in the ranks of these overseas geographic commanders, though General Lori Robinson now leads the Northern Command). They report directly to the secretary of defense and the president, with the heads of the four military services not in the chain of command and the chairman of the joint chiefs essentially in just an advisory and liaison capacity. Pacific Command is based in Hawaii; European and Africa commands are both headquartered in Europe; the others are located in the continental United States (as are the three functional commands). The four-star commanders in Korea and Afghanistan report through Pacific and Central commands, respectively. The head of European Command is also the Supreme Allied Commander of the 28-nation NATO alliance. Some of the commands had their origins in the late 1940s; most came into their current form in major reforms in either 1983, 1987 (from the Goldwater Nichols legislation), or 2002. Africa Command is the newest kid on the block, having been inaugurated in the last year of the George W. Bush administration.

All this detail should immediately underscore two crucial points: each geographic command is dramatically different from all of the others, and each commander as well as his top staff becomes as much a politician as a warfighter. These are the major reasons for being wary of reform proposals, especially those that would consolidate too much— for example, merging Africa Command with European Command or Central Command, and eliminating Southern

Command or merging it with Northern Command. Consider for a moment what several of the commands spent much of their 2015 addressing:

- General Philip Breedlove of European Command (and the U.S. Air Force himself), was focused largely on Putin, Russia, and Ukraine. He needed to track very intently the daily intelligence on what Russian, and Russian-assisted, forces were doing to stir up mischief, not only in Ukraine itself but around NATO's perimeter as well. He and his staff also needed to develop recommendations for President Obama, the Congress, and other NATO members on how to help Ukraine—and on how to deter Putin from any designs on NATO territory itself.

- General Lloyd Austin of Central Command (and the U.S. Army) needed to address a region going up in flames. He oversaw by far the most combat of any commander. Yet his job was as much about politics as military strategy—understanding Sunni-Shia tensions in Iraq, tribal rivalries in Syria and Yemen, complex internal politics in Egypt and Saudi Arabia, and the nuclear deal and all that came with it in Iran, to say nothing of Afghanistan and Pakistan (Central Command extends to the India-Pakistan border, where Pacific Command then takes over).

- General David Rodriguez of Africa Command (and the U.S. Army) was primarily in the business of working with local partners in modest training efforts. With fifty-three countries under his jurisdiction (all of Africa except Egypt), he arguably had the most complicated command of all, and his jurisdiction rivaled CENTCOM for the most ongoing hot wars. Yet unlike with CENTCOM, his area of responsibility is generally seen as a lower priority for American defense policy, and thus he had to tackle most problems with very limited resources.

- Similarly, General John Kelly of Southern Command worked with modest military resources typically at his beck and call (though the president and secretary of defense could of course assign any commander more resources in a crisis or conflict). For example, he was extremely attentive to the blossoming U.S.-Colombia relationship over his tenure, recognizing Bogota's potential to be a crucial partner for mutual hemispheric interests.

- Admiral Harry Harris of Pacific Command spent much of 2015 keeping an eagle's eye on China, and ultimately carrying out freedom-of-navigation activities with American military vessels in the South China Sea where Beijing has been building artificial islands and attempting to extend its influence. Unlike Kelly or Rodriguez, Harris had ample U.S. military assets to employ, but unlike Austin, he was not focused so much on shooting as on positioning and posturing in ways that would ideally avoid war.

So where might the case for reform in fact be compelling, beyond Dunford's and McCain's worthy goals of streamlining? To my mind, there are three main ideas that should be considered, in light of the above arguments.

First, cyber operations have reached such a high importance and complexity that arguably they should no longer be subsumed within strategic command. I do not favor creating a separate cyber service; cyber is inherent to everything that the existing services can and must do. But a separate command, focused on somewhat different questions (and more offensive options) than the National Security Agency, deserves consideration.

It is also possible to ask if Northern Command is really needed. Since Strategic Command is also focused on protecting the homeland, the idea of merging the two merits more detailed analysis.

Finally, the geographic seams of some commands may require rethinking. For example, the fact that Central Command covers Pakistan and Pacific Command covers India could complicate efforts to use the good offices of the American military to foster confidence-building measures between these two South Asian powers. Perhaps both commands should have responsibility for both countries, with a special team of Americans reporting to each commander and facilitating joint initiatives. Or perhaps this is an issue where the chairman of the joint chiefs of staff should have special responsibilities, as has often been the case in recent years. A similar case could be made for Libya, given its importance for both Central Command and Africa Command.

But the essence of the unified command structure is logical and working well and should not be revolutionized. As currently defined, the main geographic regions tend to have distinct personalities and fundamental security challenges that give them logical coherence. They also tend to encompass distinct political relationships and/or partner organizations, such as the NATO alliance, the Gulf Cooperation Council, and the African Union, with which the United States can collaborate. McCain and Dunford have identified a worthy issue—but one where careful reform rather than revolution should be the guiding principle.

CHAPTER 7

Conclusion

The case is strong for modest, sustained increases in the real-dollar levels of the U.S. national defense budget. This level of resources would fund, among other things, a "1 + 2" framework for sizing U.S. ground forces, including one major war and two sustained multilateral missions of other sorts; a robust level of Navy presence throughout the world with particularly focus on the Asia-Pacific and Persian Gulf; strong land-based deterrents and logistical infrastructures in Northeast Asia, the Persian Gulf, and Europe; a safe and reliable nuclear deterrent as well as considerable missile defense efforts including vigorous research in new technological concepts; and strong military readiness including sustained robust levels of compensation for the remarkable men and women of the American military.

The 2016 budget totals some $607 billion in new budget authority in all. That is just $5 billion short of the original Obama request for that year, and more than $30 billion in excess of levels that would have resulted had sequestration-level caps come into effect. That $607 billion includes some $27 billion for nuclear-weapons expenses in the Department of Energy and a few other various and sundry costs, $522 billion in base or core costs for the Department of Defense, and another $60 billion or so for overseas contingency operations. Under the 2015 Bipartisan Budget Act, national defense funding for 2017 is expected to total about $610 billion—with the base budget virtually unchanged from 2016, implying a slight drop in real-dollar resource levels.

The Obama budget would modestly increase that real-dollar level of the 2017 core budget through the decade, while cutting war costs dramatically (Sequestration or similar cuts, were they to recur, would leave the budget an average of about $25 billion less each year.[1]). My proposal would have the annual budget total about $650 billion in 2020 in constant 2016 dollars (again, also including war/contingency costs and the Department of Energy's nuclear weapons activities). The increase would be not so much to buy new capabilities, above and beyond what the Pentagon already intends, as to make sure we can afford the ones now fielded or planned, which tend to cost more than the Pentagon projects.

There are three main reasons for my concern that presently planned budgets will not adequately fund needed military capabilities. First, according to CBO estimates, the Obama administration may be too optimistic about the affordability of its own defense plan.[2] Second, the Army should no longer be cut; it has been reduced enough, and its size should now stabilize at about 470,000 active-duty soldiers, some 20,000 more than under current Obama plans. Third, the Obama administration has tended to be too optimistic about its ability—or its successor's ability—to hold down future expenses tied to wars and other national security crises.

My proposal, rather than count on declining overseas contingency costs, would sustain or modestly increase them through the rest of the decade. A final reason for this modest increase in real defense budgets—not a fundamental one, but an additional benefit to a modest path of real growth—is also, frankly, to habituate Congress to the fact that defense costs inherently go up faster than inflation. In most time periods, therefore, holding defense budgets flat (even in real terms) amounts to making gradual cuts in capabilities. This reality needs to be absorbed by the federal budget process and policymakers.

The U.S. national defense budget is large, but it is entirely affordable—relative to the size of the economy, relative to past levels of effort by this country in the national security domain, relative especially to the costs of failing to uphold a stable international order. It need not grow relative to GDP; indeed, by my proposals it might even decline slightly more in the years ahead. But it needs to grow faster than inflation, after a half dozen years of cutbacks. Even at a modestly higher price, it will be the best $650 billion bargain going, and a worthy investment in this country's security as well as its long-term national power.

Notes

PREFACE

1. A handy reference is Office of the Under Secretary of Defense (Comptroller), "Fiscal Year 2016 Budget Request," Washington, D.C., February 2015, available at www.comptroller.defense .gov/budgetmaterials/budget2016.aspx and the corresponding reference from February 2016 for 2017.

2. Andrew Clevenger, "Pentagon Budget Seeks to Leverage R&D Investments," *Defense News,* February 15, 2016, p. 1.

3. Mackenzie Eaglen and Rick Berger, "2017 Defense Budget: Offset Promising, but Today's Procurement Disproportionately Pays the Bills," American Enterprise Institute, Washington, D.C. (February 23, 2016).

4. It is worth noting that by 2016, the Obama administration had apparently shifted as much as $25 billion in costs previously funded out of the base budget to the OCO or supplemental budget—taking advantage of the lack of binding caps on OCO funds to use that account more liberally than in the past. Todd Harrison, "Analysis of the FY 2017 Defense Budget," Center for Strategic

and International Studies, Washington, D.C., April 2016, p. 6, available at www.sis.org/files/publication/160420_Analysis_of_the _FY2017_Defense_Budget.pdf.

CHAPTER 1

1. On the general trends, see Steven Pinker, *The Better Angels of Our Nature: Why Violence Has Declined* (New York: Penguin Books, 2011), pp. 189–294.

2. On some of these possibilities, see Robert Jervis, *Perception and Misperception in International Politics* (Princeton University Press, 1976).

3. Lotta Themnar and Peter Wallensteen, "Armed Conflict, 1946–2013," *Journal of Peace Research* 51, no. 4 (2014), available at www.pcr.uu.se/research/ucdp/charts_and_graphs; and Pinker, *The Better Angels of Our Nature,* pp. 303–04.

4. See "The Long and Short of the Problem," *The Economist,* November 9, 2013, available at www.economist.com/news/briefing /21589431-bringing-end-conflicts-within-states-vexatious-history -provides-guide.

5. Roland Paris, *At War's End: Building Peace after Civil Conflict* (Cambridge University Press, 2004); and Stephen John Stedman, Donald Rothchild, and Elizabeth M. Cousens, eds., *Ending Civil Wars: The Implementation of Peace Agreements* (Boulder, Colo.: Lynne Rienner, 2002).

6. Center on International Cooperation, *Annual Review of Global Peace Operations 2013* (New York: Lynne Rienner, 2013), p. 9.

7. See United Nations High Commissioner for Refugees, "Global Trends 2013: War's Human Cost" (New York, 2014), available at www.reliefweb.int/report/world/unhcr-global-trends-2013 -wars-human-cost.

8. RAND National Defense Research Institute Project, "Total Number of Terrorist Incidents" and "RAND Database of Worldwide Terrorism Incidents" (Santa Monica, Calif.: RAND, 2012), available at www.smapp.rand.org/rwtid/search.php.

9. David Kilcullen, *Out of the Mountains: The Coming Age of the Urban Guerrilla* (Oxford University Press, 2013); see also, on a related subject, Thomas P. M. Barnett, *The Pentagon's New Map:*

War and Peace in the Twenty-First Century (New York: G. P. Putnam's Sons, 2004).

10. Stephanie Condon, "Al Qaeda Is 'Morphing,' Not on the Run, Intel Chiefs Say," *CBS News,* February 11, 2014, available at www.cbsnews.com/news/al-qaeda-is-morphing-not-on-the-run -intel-chiefs-say.

11. See Response of Director of National Intelligence James Clapper to Question by Senator Dianne Feinstein, in "Transcript: Senate Intelligence Hearing on National Security Threats," *Washington Post,* January 29, 2014, available at www.washingtonpost .com/world/national-security/transcript-senate-intelligence -hearing-on-national-security-threats/2014/01/29/b5913184-8912 -11e3-833c-33098f9e5267_story.html.

12. L. E. Cederman, "Back to Kant: Reinterpreting the Democratic Peace as a Macrohistorical Learning Process," *American Political Science Review* 95, no. 1 (March 2001): 15–31, cited in Pinker, *The Better Angels of Our Nature,* p. 294; and Michael W. Doyle, "Kant, Liberal Legacies, and Foreign Affairs," *Philosophy and Public Affairs* 12, no. 3 (Summer 1983): 213–15.

13. See, for example, John M. Owen IV, *Liberal Peace, Liberal War: American Politics and International Security* (Cornell University Press, 1997); Shadi Hamid, *Temptations of Power: Islamists and Illiberal Democracy in a New Middle East* (Oxford University Press, 2014); Stephen R. Grand, *Understanding Tahrir Square: What Transitions Elsewhere Can Teach Us about the Prospects for Arab Democracy* (Brookings, 2014), p. 15; Freedom House, "The Democratic Leadership Gap" (Washington, D.C., 2014), available at www.freedomhouse.org/sites/default/files/Overview%20Fact %20Sheet.pdf; and John J. Mearsheimer, *The Tragedy of Great Power Relations* (New York: W. W. Norton, 2001).

14. See Bruce Jones, Testimony before the Senate Foreign Relations Committee, "U.N. Peacekeeping and Opportunities for Reform," December 9, 2015, available at www.brookings.edu/research /testimony/2015/12/09-un-peacekeeping-opportunities-jones.

15. See, for example, Lawrence Freedman, *The Evolution of Nuclear Strategy* (New York: St. Martin's Press, 1981); Thomas C. Schelling, *The Strategy of Conflict* (Harvard University Press,

1960); Thomas C. Schelling, *Arms and Influence* (Yale University Press, 1966); Barry R. Posen, *Inadvertent Escalation: Conventional War and Nuclear Risks* (Cornell University Press, 1991); Bruce G. Blair, *Strategic Command and Control: Redefining the Nuclear Threat* (Brookings, 1985); Michael Dobbs, *One Minute to Midnight: Kennedy, Khrushchev, and Castro on the Brink of Nuclear War* (New York: Alfred A. Knopf, 2008); McGeorge Bundy, *Danger and Survival: Choices about the Bomb in the First Fifty Years* (New York: Vintage Books, 1988); Robert Jervis, *The Illogic of American Nuclear Strategy* (Cornell University Press, 1984); Frederick Kempe, *Berlin 1961: Kennedy, Khrushchev, and the Most Dangerous Place on Earth* (New York: G. P. Putnam's Sons, 2011); and Richard K. Betts, *Nuclear Blackmail and Nuclear Balance* (Brookings, 1987).

16. See, for example, Francois Heisbourg, "Nuclear Proliferation—Looking Back, Thinking Ahead: How Bad Would the Further Spread of Nuclear Weapons Be?" in *Moving Beyond Pretense: Nuclear Power and Nonproliferation,* edited by Henry Sokolski (Carlisle, Pa.: Strategic Studies Institute, U.S. Army War College, 2014), pp. 17–43.

17. See, for example, Geoffrey Blainey, *The Causes of War* (New York: Free Press, 1973), pp. 247–49; and John Keegan, *The First World War* (New York: Alfred A. Knopf, 1999).

18. John Mueller, *Atomic Obsession: Nuclear Alarmism from Hiroshima to Al-Qaeda* (Oxford University Press, 2010), pp. 29–42.

19. On these issues, see, for example, John D. Steinbruner, *Principles of Global Security* (Brookings, 2000); Bruce Jones, Carlos Pascual, and Stephen John Stedman, *Power and Responsibility: Building International Order in an Era of Transnational Threats* (Brookings, 2009); Anthony Lake, *Six Nightmares: Real Threats in a Dangerous World and How America Can Meet Them* (Boston: Little, Brown, 2000); Graham Allison, *Nuclear Terrorism: The Ultimate Preventable Catastrophe* (New York: Henry Holt, 2004); and Matthew Bunn, Martin B. Malin, Nickolas Roth, and William H. Tobey, *Advancing Nuclear Security: Evaluating Progress and Setting New Goals* (Harvard University Press, 2014).

20. For example, Richard Betts of Columbia (and a number of others) argued strongly against NATO expansion in the 1990s on

the ground that it could isolate, embitter, and provoke Russia—though few if any of those scholars have gone so far as to assert that the U.S./NATO decisions of that era provided a legitimate rationale for Vladimir Putin to act as he did in Georgia in 2008 and in Ukraine in 2014. See Richard K. Betts, *American Force: Dangers, Delusions, and Dilemmas in National Security* (Columbia University Press, 2012), pp. 189–98. More recently, Barry Posen has argued that U.S. alliance commitments, generally viewed as stabilizing because they help reassure many countries that might otherwise build up large militaries or acquire nuclear weapons to ensure their security, may embolden some of these countries to behave more assertively and thus more dangerously than they otherwise would. But his main concern is that the United States pays excessive costs because of primacy, not that the world has become fundamentally more dangerous as a result of U.S. actions. See Posen, *Restraint.* See also Campbell Craig, Benjamin H. Friedman, Brendan Rittenhouse Green, and Justin Logan, as well as Stephen G. Brooks, G. John Ikenberry, and William C. Wohlforth, "Correspondence—Debating American Engagement: The Future of U.S. Grand Strategy," *International Security* 38, no. 2 (Fall 2013): 181–99.

21. Michael Mastanduno, "Preserving the Unipolar Moment: Realist Theories and U.S. Grand Strategy after the Cold War," *International Security* 21, no. 4 (Spring 1997): 49–88.

CHAPTER 2

1. Congressional Budget Office, *Growth in DoD's Budget from 2000 to 2014* (Washington, D.C., 2014), p. 1, available at www.cbo.gov/publication/49764.

2. See William J. Perry, John P. Abizaid, and others, *Ensuring a Strong U.S. Defense for the Future* (Washington, D.C.: National Defense Panel, 2014), p. 4, available at www.usip.org/sites/default/files/Ensuring-a-Strong-U.S.-Defense-for-the-Future-NDP-Review-of-the-QDR_0.pdf.

3. President Barack Obama, "State of the Union Address," Washington, D.C., January 12, 2016, available at www.whitehouse.gov/the-press-office/2016/01/12/remarks-president-barack-obama-%E2%80%93-prepared-delivery-state-union-address.

4. See Jennifer H. Svan, "USAFE Chief: Russian Air Defenses No. 1 Concern," *Stars and Stripes,* December 11, 2015, p. 2.

5. Committee for a Responsible Federal Budget, "Analysis of CBO's January 2016 Budget and Economic Outlook," Washington, D.C., January 26, 2016, available at www.crfb.org/document /analysis-cbos-january-2016-budget-and-economic-outlook.

CHAPTER 3

1. Eric Heginbotham and others, *The U.S.-China Military Scorecard* (Santa Monica, Calif.: RAND, 2015), pp. 323–24.

2. Andrew Tate, "PLA to Undergo Major Structural Reforms," *Jane's Defence Weekly,* December 9, 2015, p. 7.

3. See James Steinberg and Michael O'Hanlon, *Strategic Reassurance and Resolve: U.S.-China Relations in the 21st Century* (Princeton University Press, 2014), p. 93.

4. Remarks by Secretary of Defense Leon Panetta at IISS Asia Security Summit, Shangri-La Hotel, Singapore, June 2, 2012, www.cfr.org/asia/panettas-speech-shangri-la-security-dialogue -june-2012/p28435.

5. Remarks by Secretary of Defense Chuck Hagel at IISS Asia Security Summit, Shangri-La Hotel, Singapore, June 1, 2013, www .defense.gov/transcripts/transcript.aspx?transcriptid=5251; Ashton Carter, "The U.S. Strategic Rebalance to Asia: A Defense Perspective," in Aspen Institute Congressional Program Paper Series, *South Asia: Policy Challenges for the U.S.* 28, no. 1 (February 16–24, 2013).

6. Robert Blackwill, Kurt Campbell, *Xi Jinping on the Global Stage: Chinese Foreign Policy Under a Powerful but Exposed Leader* (New York: Council on Foreign Relations, 2016).

7. Ellis Joffe, "The 'Right Size' for China's Military: To What Ends?" in Roy Kamphausen and Andrew Scobell, eds., *Right-Sizing the People's Liberation Army: Exploring the Contours of China's Military* (Carlisle, Pa.: Strategic Studies Institute, 2007), p. 570. A 60-40 split in the submarine force was announced in 2006; see Secretary of Defense Donald Rumsfeld, *Quadrennial Defense Review Report* (February 6, 2006), p. 47.

8. On the Army, Vietnam, and Vietnam's aftermath, see, for example, Andrew F. Krepinevich Jr., *The Army and Vietnam*

(Johns Hopkins University Press, 1986); John A. Nagl, *Knife Fights: A Memoir of Modern War in Theory and Practice* (New York: Penguin Press, 2014), pp. 212–13; and David Fitzgerald, *Learning to Forget: U.S. Army Counterinsurgency Doctrine and Practice from Vietnam to Iraq* (Stanford University Press, 2013). On more recent wars, see Gian Gentile, *Wrong Turn: America's Deadly Embrace of Counterinsurgency* (New York: New Press, 2013).

9. President Barack Obama, introductory remarks to "Sustaining U.S. Global Leadership: Priorities for 21st Century Defense" (Department of Defense, January 2012), available at www .defense.gov/news/defense_strategic_guidance.pdf.

10. See, for example, Max Boot, *Invisible Armies: An Epic History of Guerrilla Warfare from Ancient Times to the Present* (New York: Liveright Publishing Co., 2012); see also Russell F. Weigley, *The American Way of War* (Indiana University Press, 1973); and Fred Kaplan, *The Insurgents: David Petraeus and the Plot to Change the American Way of War* (New York: Simon and Schuster, 2013).

11. Conrad C. Crane, "The Lure of Strike," *Parameters* 43, no. 2 (Summer 2013): 1–12.

12. "General David H. Petraeus's Retirement Ceremony Remarks," Washington, D.C., August 31, 2011, available at www .army.mil/article/64706/Gen__David_H__Petraeus__retirement _ceremony_remarks.

13. Carol Kerr, "CSA Discusses Army Operating Concept with Army War College Class of 2015," September 8, 2014, available at www.army.mil/article/133303/CSA_discusses_Army_Operating _Concept_with_Army_War_College_class_of_2015.

14. Thom Shanker, "Win Wars? Today's Generals Must Also Politick and Do P.R.," *New York Times,* August 12, 2010, available at www.nytimes.com/2010/08/13/world/13generals.html ?pagewanted=all.

15. The First Armored Division from Fort Bliss, Texas, was in Afghanistan, and the First Cavalry Division from Fort Hood, Texas, was in Korea. See www.army.mil/article/132943/1st_Cavalry _unit_selected_for_South_Korea_deployment. The First Infantry Division from Fort Riley, Kansas, was in the CENTCOM/Persian

Gulf theater. See www.army.mil/article/134543/1st_Infantry _Division_HQ_deploying_to_Iraq. The Second Infantry Division was as usual at Camp Casey in South Korea; see www .facebook.com/2IDKorea. The Third Infantry Division, from Fort Stewart, Georgia, was in Afghanistan; see www.army.mil/article /137188/3ID_HQ_to_deploy_to_Afghanistan_as_drawdown_ _retrograde_continues. The Fourth Infantry Division, from Fort Carson, Colorado, was not deployed (www.facebook.com /MountainWarriorBrigade). The Tenth Mountain Division, from Fort Drum, New York, was in Afghanistan (www.drum.army.mil /news/Home.aspx). The Twenty-Fifth Infantry Division, from Schofield Barracks in Hawaii, was headed to Korea in 2015 (www .army.mil/article/139140/). The Eighty-Second Airborne Division, from Fort Bragg, North Carolina, was heading out to the CENT- COM/Gulf theater shortly (www.armytimes.com/story/military /pentagon/2014/12/01/about-250-fort-bragg-soldiers-deploy -support-iraq-operations/19741789/). The 101st Airborne Division, from Fort Campbell, Kentucky, was in Liberia www.military.com /daily-news/2014/09/30/101st-airborne-troops-headed-to-liberia -in-ebola-fight.html.

16. Quoted in Thomas S. Szayna, Derek Eaton, and Amy Richardson, *Preparing the Army for Stability Operations* (Santa Monica, Calif.: RAND, 2007), p. 10.

17. John A. Nagl, *Learning to Eat Soup with a Knife* (University of Chicago Press, 2002).

18. See, for example, Melissa McAdam, "Military Advising After Afghanistan," *Marine Corps Gazette* (August 2014), pp. 55–58.

19. See, for example, David. C. Gompert, John Gordon IV, Adam Grisson, David R. Frelinger, Seth G. Jones, Martin C. Libicki, Edward O'Connell, Brooke K. Stearns, and Robert E. Hunter, *War by Other Means: Building Complete and Balanced Capabilities for Counterinsurgency* (Santa Monica, Calif.: RAND, 2008); and Robert M. Perito, *Where Is the Lone Ranger: America's Search for a Stability Force,* 2d ed. (Washington, D.C.: U.S. Institute of Peace, 2013).

20. See, for example, David W. Barno, "The Army's Next Enemy? Peace," *Washington Post,* July 13, 2014, p. B1.

21. See, for example, Bernard Rostker, *I Want You! The Evolution of the All-Volunteer Force* (Santa Monica, Calif.: RAND, 2006); Thomas E. Ricks, *Making the Corps* (New York: Simon and Schuster, 1997); and Bruce Newsome, *Made, Not Born: Why Some Soldiers Are Better Than Others* (Westport, Conn.: Praeger, 2007).

22. Sam Jones, "Cameron Embarks on Big Military Expansion," *Financial Times,* November 24, 2015, p. 6.

23. See, for example, Gary J. Schmitt, "Introduction," in Gary J. Schmitt, ed., *A Hard Look at Hard Power: Assessing the Defense Capabilities of Key U.S. Allies and Security Partners* (Carlisle, Pa.: Strategic Studies Institute, U.S. Army War College, 2015), p. 3.

24. This was a key emphasis of Secretary of Defense Leon Panetta, among others. See the discussion of his June 2012 speech on building partnerships in Richard L. Kugler and Linton Wells II, *Strategic Shift: Appraising Recent Changes in U.S. Defense Plans and Priorities* (National Defense University, 2013), pp. 67–75.

25. Dennis Blair, *Military Engagement: Influencing Armed Forces Worldwide to Support Democratic Transitions:* Vol. 1: *Overview and Action Plan* (Brookings, 2013), p. 59.

26. Michael J. Lostumbo and others, *Overseas Basing of U.S. Military Forces: An Assessment of Relative Costs and Strategic Benefits* (Santa Monica, Calif.: RAND, 2013).

27. John R. Deni, *The Future of American Landpower: Does Forward Presence Still Matter? The Case of the Army in Europe* (Carlisle, Pa.: Strategic Studies Institute, U.S. Army War College, 2012), pp. 10, 34.

CHAPTER 4

1. It is largely on this matter that the Heritage Foundation reached a more alarming assessment of the strength of the U.S. military than I do here—while Heritage did have some concerns about the readiness of individual units, some of which I share and some of which I do not, it continually returned to the issue of size and overall capacity in reaching its conclusions. See Dakota L. Wood, ed., *2016 Index of U.S. Military Strength: Assessing America's Ability to Provide for the Common Defense* (Washington, D.C.: Heritage, 2015), pp. 12–14.

2. For an excellent and thorough discussion of this issue, see Robert F. Hale, "Budgetary Turmoil at the Department of Defense from 2010 to 2014: A Personal and Professional Journey," Brookings Institution Paper, Washington, D.C., August 2015, available at www.brookings.edu/research/papers/2015/08/budget-turmoil -defense-department-hale.

3. Office of the Under Secretary of Defense (Comptroller), "United States Department of Defense Fiscal Year 2016 Budget Request, Overview," Department of Defense, Washington, D.C., February 2015, pp. 3–1 through 3–15, available at comptroller .defense.gov/budgetmaterials/budget2016.aspx. These figures were essentially unchanged in the FY 2017 budget proposal.

4. Vice Admiral Bill Moran, "Health of the Force: CY14 End of Year Executive Summary," Department of the Navy, Washington, D.C., January 2015, p. 56.

5. For a similar view, though one also sharing my concerns about various challenges and problems, see Mackenzie Eaglen, *State of the U.S. Military: A Defense Primer* (Washington, D.C.: American Enterprise Institute, October 2015) pp. 22–25, available at www .aei.org/publication/state-of-the-us-military-a-defense-primer; for a paper expressing some concerns about trends in the academic aptitude of Marine Corps officers, however, see Matthew F. Cancian and Michael W. Klein, "Military Officer Quality in the All-Volunteer Force" (Brookings Institution, July 2015), available at www.brookings.edu/~/media/research/files/papers/2015/07/20 -military-officer-quality/military-officer-quality-in-the-all -volunteer-force.pdf.

6. Office of the Under Secretary of Defense, Personnel and Readiness, *Population Representation in the Military Services, 2014* (Department of Defense, 2014), available at www.cna.org /pop-rep/2014/appendixd/d_08.html.

7. Center for Naval Analyses, "Attrition and Reenlistment of First-Term Sailors" (Alexandria, Virginia: 2015).

8. Department of Defense, *2014 Demographics: Profile of the Military Community* (Department of Defense, 2014), available at www.download.militaryonesource.mil/12038/MOS/Reports /2014-Demographics-Report.pdf.

9. Vice Admiral Bill Moran, "Health of the Force: CY14 End of Year Executive Summary," Department of the Navy, Washington, D.C., January 2015, p. 43.

10. David Barno and Nora Bensahel, "Can the U.S. Military Halt Its Brain Drain?" *The Atlantic,* November 5, 2015, available at www.theatlantic.com/politics/archive/2015/11/us-military-tries -halt-brain-drain/413965.

11. Mike Mochizuki and Michael O'Hanlon, "Solving the Okinawa Problem," *Foreignpolicy.com,* October 12, 2012, available at www.brookings.edu/research/opinions/2012/10/12-okinawa -japan-us-military-ohanlon.

12. Robert P. Haffa, Jr., *Rational Methods, Prudent Choices: Planning U.S. Forces* (Washington, D.C.: National Defense University, 1988), pp. 77–82, 110–26; Alain C. Enthoven and K. Wayne Smith, *How Much Is Enough?: Shaping the Defense Program 1961– 1969* (Santa Monica, Calif.: RAND, 2005, original publication date 1971), pp. 214–16; John Lewis Gaddis, *Strategies of Containment* (Oxford University Press, 1982), pp. 297, 323.

13. See Gaddis, *Strategies of Containment.*

14. For discussions of the force-sizing debates in this period, see, for example, Kagan, *Finding the Target,* pp. 196–97, 281–86; and Michael E. O'Hanlon, *Defense Policy Choices for the Bush Administration,* 2d ed. (Brookings, 2002), pp. 9–17, 63–71.

15. William Stueck, "Revisionism and the Korean War," *Journal of Conflict Studies,* vol. 22, no. 1 (Spring 2002), available at www.journals.hil.unb.ca/index.php/jcs/article/view/365/576.

16. See, for example, Mike Winnerstig, ed., *Tools of Destabilization: Russian Soft Power and Non-Military Influence in the Baltic States* (Stockholm, Sweden: FOI, 2014); and Senator Jack Reed, "Trip Report: Belgium, Ukraine and Turkey," September 2015.

17. On Putin, see Fiona Hill and Clifford G. Gaddy, *Mr. Putin: Operative in the Kremlin* (Brookings, 2015).

18. Tara Copp, "Ukraine and Syria Giving U.S. Glimpse into Russian Tactics," *Stars and Stripes,* December 11, 2015, p. 3.

19. Michael Evans, "U.S. Readies 5,000 More Troops to Deter Putin," *Times of London,* March 8, 2016, p. 31.

20. Elbridge Colby and Jonathan Solomon, "Facing Russia: Conventional Defense and Deterrence in Europe," *Survival,* vol. 57, no. 6 (December 2015–January 2016), pp. 31–43; and Matthew Kroenig, "Facing Reality: Getting NATO Ready for a New Cold War," *Survival,* vol. 57, no. 1 (February–March 2015), pp. 49–70.

21. See, for example, J. Randy Forbes, "The U.S. Army Should Pursue a Counter-A2/AD Mission," *National Interest,* available at www.nationalinterest.org/feature/the-us-army-should-pursue -counter-a2-ad-mission-11486.

22. Elbridge Colby, "Preparing for Limited War," *National Interest,* no. 140 (November/December 2015), pp. 11–22.

23. See Michael E. O'Hanlon, *The Future of Land Warfare* (Brookings, 2015).

24. National Commission on the Future of the Army, *Report of the National Commission on the Future of the Army* (Washington, D.C.: January 2016), pp. 2, 53–55, available at www.ncfa.ncr .gov/media.

25. James Steinberg and Michael E. O'Hanlon, *Strategic Reassurance and Resolve: U.S.-China Relations in the Twenty-First Century* (Princeton University Press, 2014), p. 94.

26. Bryan Clark, "Deploying Beyond Their Means: The U.S. Navy and Marine Corps at a Tipping Point," *Nationalinterest.org,* November 18, 2015, available at www.nationalinterest.org/feature /deploying-beyond-their-means-the-us-navy-marine-corps -14378.

27. Moran, "Health of the Force," p. 46.

28. Barbara Starr, "U.S. Won't Have Aircraft Carrier in Persian Gulf for at least Two Months," *CNN.com,* August 6, 2015, available at www.cnn.com/2015/08/05/politics/no-aircraft-carrier -persian-gulf-iran.

29. Eric J. Labs, *An Analysis of the Navy's Fiscal Year 2016 Shipbuilding Plan* (Washington, D.C.: Congressional Budget Office, October 2015), p. 1, available at www.cbo.gov/publication/50926; David Adesnik, "FPI Bulletin: Relief for an Overextended Navy," Foreign Policy Initiative, Washington, D.C., February 22, 2016, available at www.foreignpolicyi.org/content/fpi-bulletin-relief -overextended-navy; and Bryan Clark and Jesse Sloman, "Deploy-

ing Beyond Their Means: America's Navy and Marine Corps at a Tipping Point," Center for Strategic and Budgetary Assessments, Washington, D.C., November 18, 2015, available at www.csbaonline .org/publications/2015/11/deploying-beyond-their-means -americas-navy-and-marine-corps-at-a-tipping-point.

30. Testimony of Eric J. Labs, Congressional Budget Office, before the Subcommittee on Seapower and Projection Forces, House Armed Services Committee, December 1, 2015, p. 5, available at www.cbo.gov/sites/default/files/114th-congress-2015-2016/reports /50981-ShipbuildingTestimony.pdf.

31. See comments of Secretary of the Navy Ray Mabus, Brookings Institution, Washington, D.C., February 26, 2016, available at www.brookings.edu/events/2016/02/26-maritime-strategy-new -era-of-naval-challenges.

32. Testimony of Eric J. Labs, Congressional Budget Office, before the Subcommittee on Seapower and Projection Forces, House Armed Services Committee, December 1, 2015, p. 30, available at www.cbo.gov/sites/default/files/114th-congress-2015-2016 /reports/50981-ShipbuildingTestimony.pdf.

33. Christopher P. Cavas, "General Dynamics: We Need Navy's Answers on SSBN(X) Subs Acquisition Plan," *Defense News,* October 5, 2015, available at www.defensenews.com/story/defense -news/2015/10/05/ohio-replacement-submarine-orp-ssbnx -newport-news-electric-boat-general-dynamics-navy-john-casey -mike-petters-hii-huntington-ingalls-industries/73181904.

34. See comments of Admiral John Richardson, Brookings Institution, Washington, D.C., February 26, 2016, available at www .brookings.edu/events/2016/02/26-maritime-strategy-new-era-of -naval-challenges.

35. Representative J. Randy Forbes, "Not Enough Subs, so Buy More," breakingdefense.com, March 8, 2016, available at www .breakingdefense.com/2016/03/not-enough-subs-so-buy-more -rep-forbes.

36. Government Accountability Office, "Defense Acquisitions: Assessments of Selected Weapon Programs," Washington, D.C., March 2015, pp. 87–88, 105–106, available at www.gao.gov/assets /670/668986.pdf.

37. John McCain, "The Real Arctic Threat," *Wall Street Journal,* September 1, 2015, available at www.wsj.com/articles/the-real-arctic-threat-1441149448.

38. Paul Scharre, "Robotics on the Battlefield, Part I: Range, Persistence, and Daring," Center for a New American Security, Washington, D.C., May 2014, pp. 19–30; and Seth Cropsey, Bryan G. McGrath, and Timothy A. Walton, "Sharpening the Spear: The Carrier, the Joint Force, and High-End Conflict," Hudson Institute, Washington, D.C., October 2015, pp. 63–80, available at www.hudson.org/research/11731-sharpening-the-spear-the-carrier-the-joint-force-and-high-end-conflict.

39. Office of the Under Secretary of Defense (Comptroller), "Fiscal Year 2017 Budget Request: Briefing Slides," February 2016, available at www.comptroller.defense.gov/budgetmaterials/budget2017.aspx.

40. Statement of Christine H. Fox, Director of Cost Assessment and Program Evaluation, Department of Defense, before the Senate Armed Services Committee, May 19, 2011, available at www.armed-services.senate.gov/e_witnesslist.cfm?id=5213 (accessed August 1, 2011); and Andrea Shalal-Ela, "Exclusive: U.S. Sees Lifetime Cost of F-35 Fighter at $1.45 Trillion," Reuters, March 29, 2012, available at www.reuters.com/article/2012/03/29/us-lockheed-fighter-idUSBRE82S03L20120329.

41. See Statement of General James F. Amos before the House Armed Services Committee on the 2011 Posture of the United States Marine Corps, March 1, 2011, p. 13, available at www.armedservices.house.gov/index.cfm/files/serve?File_id=6e6d479e-0bea-41a1-8f3d-44b3147640fe (accessed August 10, 2011).

42. See Captain Henry J. Hendicks and Lt. Col. J. Noel Williams, "Twilight of the Superfluous Carrier," *Proceedings* (May 2011), available at www.usni.org (accessed May 3, 2011).

43. Northrop Grumman, "X-47B UCAS," Washington, D.C., 2013, available at www.as.northropgrumman.com/products/nucasx47b/index.html. An additional virtue of unmanned systems is the ability to conduct training for pilots less expensively.

44. These are ongoing; see Bill Carey, "F-35 Delay Forces $3 Billion Upgrade Request for U.S. Air Force F-16s," AINOnline,

November 4, 2011, available at www.ainonline.com/aviation-news /ain-defense-perspective/2011-11-04/f-35-delay-forces-3-billion -upgrade-request-us-air-force-f-16s.

45. See U.S. Air Force, Fact Sheet on MQ-9 Reaper, January 2012, available at www.af.mil/information/factsheets/factsheet .asp?id=6405; and Congressional Budget Office, *Policy Options for Unmanned Aerial Systems* (Washington, D.C., June 2011), pp. ix– x, available at www.cbo.gov (accessed August 13, 2011).

46. Leithen Francis, "Mission Impossible," *Aviation Week and Space Technology,* August 15, 2011, p. 27.

47. The Chief of Naval Operations, while not abandoning support for the F-35C, has nonetheless voiced some doubts over the central role of stealth in future force planning. See Admiral Jonathan W. Greenert, "Payloads over Platforms: Charting a New Course," *Proceedings,* vol. 138, no. 7 (July 2012), available at www. usni.org/magazines/proceedings/2012-07/payloads-over -platforms-charting-new-course.

48. Congressional Budget Office, *Projected Costs of U.S. Nuclear Forces, 2015 to 2024* (Washington, D.C., 2015), available at www.cbo.gov/publication/49870.

49. Kingston Reif, "Hill Denies Money for Submarine Fund," *Arms Control Today,* vol. 46, no. 1 (January/February 2016), pp. 45–47.

50. See Michael O'Hanlon, *A Skeptic's Case for Nuclear Disarmament* (Brookings, 2010).

51. See Sean M. Maloney, "Remembering Soviet Nuclear Risks," *Survival,* vol. 57, no. 4 (August–September 2014); Gregory D. Koblentz, "Command and Combust: America's Secret History of Atomic Accidents," *Foreign Affairs,* vol. 93, no. 1 (January/February 2014), pp. 167–72; and Lawrence J. Cavaiola, David C. Gompert, and Martin Libicki, "Cyber House Rules: On War, Retaliation and Escalation," *Survival,* vol. 57, no. 1 (February–March 2015), pp. 86–87.

52. On this kind of idea, see, for example Stephen M. Younger, *The Bomb: A New History* (New York: Ecco Books, 2010); and Wallace R. Turnbull III, "Time to Come in from the Cold (War)," *Joint Forces Quarterly,* issue 79 (2015), pp. 38–45.

53. Labs, *An Analysis of the Navy's Fiscal Year 2016 Shipbuilding Plan,* p. 12.

54. Lauren Caston, Robert S. Leonard, Christopher A. Mouton, Chad J.R. Ohlandt, S. Craig Moore, Raymond E. Conley, and Glenn Buchan, *The Future of the U.S. Intercontinental Ballistic Missile Force* (Santa Monica, Calif.: RAND, 2014), available at www.rand.org/pubs/monographs/M61210.html.

55. See Steven Pifer, "Who Needs a New Nuclear Air-Launched Cruise Missile Anyway?," *Order from Chaos* blog, Brookings Institution, Washington, D.C., December 10, 2015, available at www .brookings.edu/blogs/order-from-chaos/posts/2015/12/10-long -range-stand-off-weapon-unnecessary-pifer.

56. Daryl G. Kimball, "The U.S. Nuclear Weapons Spending Binge," *Arms Control Today,* vol. 45, no. 10 (December 2015), p. 3.

57. Labs, *An Analysis of the Navy's Fiscal Year 2016 Shipbuilding Plan,* p. 17; Pifer, "Who Needs a New Nuclear Air-Launched Cruise Missile Anyway?;" and Michael E. O'Hanlon, *The Science of War* (Princeton University Press, 2009), p. 28.

58. On Guam, see Andrew S. Erickson and Justin D. Mikolay, "Guam and American Security in the Pacific," in Carnes Lord and Andrew S. Erickson, eds., *Rebalancing U.S. Forces: Basing and Forward Presence in the Asia-Pacific* (Annapolis, Md.: Naval Institute Press, 2014), pp. 15–35.

59. Kelley Sayler, "Red Alert: The Growing Threat to U.S. Aircraft Carriers," Center for a New American Security, Washington, D.C., February 2016, available at www.cnas.org/sites /default/files/publications-pdf/CNASReport-CarrierThreat -160217.pdf.

60. Vice Admiral James Syring, Missile Defense Agency, "Ballistic Missile Defense System Update," Center for Strategic and International Studies, Washington, D.C., January 19, 2016, available at www.csis.org/event/ballistic-missile-defense-system-update; General Paul Selva, Vice Chairman of the Joint Chiefs of Staff, "Trends in Military Technology and the Future Force," Brookings Institution, Washington, D.C., January 21, 2016, available at www .brookings.edu/~/media/events/2016/01/21-military-technology /20160121_selva_military_tech_transcript.pdf.

61. Lockheed Martin, "Briefing: Integrated Air and Missile Defense and Changing Global Security Needs," Arlington, VA, October 29, 2015.

CHAPTER 5

1. Warren Strobel and Mark Hosenball, "Islamic State Unlikely to be Ejected from Mosul in 2016: U.S. General," *Reuters,* February 9, 2016, available at www.reuters.com/article/us-mideast-crisis-usa-mosul-idUSKCN0VI25G.

2. Michael O'Hanlon and Amy Copley, "How the West Can Do More Militarily in Africa," *Foresight Africa: Top Priorities for the Continent in 2015* (Brookings, 2015), pp. 15–18.

3. See Department of Defense, "Enhancing Security and Stability in Afghanistan," Washington, D.C., December 2015, pp. 17–22, available at www.defense.gov/Portals/1/Documents/pubs/1225 _Report_Dec_2015-_Final_20151210.pdf, for these and other trends in the security situation. See also, Ian Livingston and Michael O'Hanlon, "The Afghanistan Index," December 2015, available at www.brookings.edu/afghanistanindex.

4. The Asia Foundation, "A Survey of the Afghan People," San Francisco, 2015, pp. 5–13, available at www.asiafoundation.org /resources/pdfs/Afghanistanin2015.pdf.

5. See David Petraeus and Michael O'Hanlon, "Unleash U.S. Airpower in Afghanistan," *Washington Post,* January 15, 2016, p. A21.

6. See, for example, Will McCants, "Why ISIS Really Wants to Conquer Baghdad," Brookings blog, November 12, 2014, available at www.brookings.edu/blogs/markaz/posts/2014/11/12-baghdad -of-al-rashid-mccants.

7. Frederick W. Kagan, Kimberly Kagan, Jennifer Cafarella, Harleen Gambhir, and Katherine Zimmerman, "Al Qaeda and ISIS: Existential Threats to the U.S. and Europe," Washington, D.C., Institute for the Study of War, 2016, available at www .understandingwar.org/report/al-qaeda-and-isis-existential -threats-us-and-europe.

8. Cody Poplin, "George Washington University Releases 'ISIS in America' Report and Material Support Database," *Lawfare,*

December 4, 2015, available at www.lawfareblog.com/george
-washington-university-releases-isis-america-report-and-material
-support-database.

9. See Emile Hokayem, *Syria's Uprising and the Fracturing of
the Levant* (London: International Institute for Strategic Studies,
2013), p. 17; and Jessica Stern and J.M. Berger, *ISIS: The State of
Terror* (New York: HarperCollins, 2015).

10. Associated Press, "U.S. Official: Airstrikes Killed 10,000
Islamic State Fighters," *New York Times,* June 3, 2015, available at
www.nytimes.com/aponline/2015/06/03/world/middleeast/ap-ml
-islamic-state.html?ref=world.

11. The Honorable James R. Clapper, "IC's Worldwide Threat
Assessment," Senate Armed Services Committee, Washington, D.C.,
February 9, 2016, available at www.dni.gov/files/documents/2016-02
-09SASC_open_threat_hearing_transcript.pdf.

CHAPTER 6

1. Bruce Newsome, *Made, Not Born: Why Some Soldiers Are
Better than Others* (Westport, Conn.: Praeger, 2007). Some changes
are already being made to reduce training modestly; see "Operational Training Rates," *Air Force Magazine* (April 2011), p. 69.

2. Department of Defense, *Report of the Eleventh Quadrennial
Review of Military Compensation* (2012), pp. 26–29, available at
www.Militarypay.defense.gov/REPORTS/QRMC/11th_QRMC
_Main_Report_Linked.pdf.

3. Congressional Budget Office, "Costs of Military Pay and
Benefits in the Defense Budget," Washington, D.C., November
2012, p. 2, available at www.cbo.gov.

4. According to Blue Star Families, 55 percent of active-duty
spouses are not employed, and a majority of that group would like
to have work. See Blue Star Families, "2015 Annual Military
Family Lifestyle Survey," San Diego, California, October 2015,
available at www.bluestarfam.org/resources/military-family-lifestyle
-survey.

5. Congressional Budget Office, *Budget Options,* pp. 28–29.

6. See Secretary of Defense Robert M. Gates, Remarks at
American Enterprise Institute, May 24, 2011, available at www.aei

.org (accessed August 1, 2011); Congressional Budget Office, *The Effects of Proposals to Increase Cost-Sharing in TRICARE* (Washington, D.C.: 2009), p. 4; and Karl Gingrich, "Making It Personnel: The Need for Military Compensation Reform," Brookings Institution, Washington, D.C., February 2012, available at www.brookings.edu/~/media/research/files/papers/2012/2/military%20compensation%20gingrich/02_military_compensation_gingrich.pdf.

7. Defense Business Board, "Modernizing the Military Retirement System," July 21, 2011, p. 18, available at www.slideshare.net/BrianLucke/modernizing-the-military-retirement-system (accessed August 5, 2011).

8. For a summary of the panel, see Michael O'Hanlon, "A Systematic Use of Performance-Based Logistics Will Save DoD Money," Brookings Institution, Washington, D.C., October, 2014, available at www.brookings.edu/blogs/up-front/posts/2014/10/15-performance-based-logistics.

9. Government Accountability Office, "Strategic Sourcing: Improved and Expanded Use Could Save Billions in Annual Procurement Costs," GAO-12-919, September 2012, pp. 11–13, available at www.gao.org/assets/383/186231.pdf.

10. Government Accountability Office, "Military Base Realignments and Closures: Updated Costs and Savings Estimates from BRAC 2005," GAO-12-709R, June 29, 2012, pp. 1–5, available at www.gao.gov/assets/600/592076.pdf.

11. Tadlock Cowan, "Military Base Closures: Socioeconomic Impacts," Congressional Research Service, February 7, 2012, available at www.fas.org/sgp/crs/natsec/RS22147.pdf; and Department of Defense, "Base Structure Report—Fiscal Year 2015 Baseline," Washington, D.C., 2015, pp. 4–18, available at www.kritisches-netzwerk.de/sites/default/files/US%20Department%20of%20Defense%20-%20Base%20Structure%20Report%20Fiscal%20Year%202015%20Baseline%20-%20As%20of%2030%20Sept%202014%20-%20A%20Summary%20of%20the%20Real%20Property%20Inventory%20-%20206%20pages_5.pdf.

12. Statement of Robert F. Hale, Under Secretary of Defense for Financial Management and Comptroller, Brookings Institution, Washington, D.C., January 7, 2013.

13. For historical perspective, see, for example, G. Wayne Glass, "Closing Military Bases: An Interim Assessment," Congressional Budget Office, Washington, D.C., December 1996, p. 63.

14. Ashton B. Carter, "Running the Pentagon Right: How to Get the Troops What They Need," *Foreign Affairs,* vol. 93, no. 1 (January/February 2014), pp. 101–12.

15. See William J. Lynn, "The End of the Military-Industrial Complex: How the Pentagon Is Adapting to Globalization," *Foreign Affairs,* vol. 93, no. 6 (November/December 2014), pp. 104–10.

16. James A. Winnefeld, Christopher Kirchhoff, and David M. Upton, "Cybersecurity's Human Factor: Lessons from the Pentagon," *Harvard Business Review* (September 2015), available at www.hbr.org/2015/09/cybersecuritys-human-factor-lessons-from -the-pentagon.

CHAPTER 7

1. For sources of these and a number of other figures used in this paper, see Office of the Under Secretary of Defense (Comptroller), "Fiscal Year 2016 Budget Request," Washington, D.C., February 2015, available at www.comptroller.defense.gov/budget materials/budget2016.aspx.

2. Congressional Budget Office, *Long-Term Implications of the 2015 Future Years Defense Program* (Washington, D.C.: November 2014), p. 2, available at www.cbo.gov/sites/default/files/113th-congress-2013-2014/reports/49483-FDYP.pdf.

Index